Praise for
Chakra Rituals

"Cristi brings a new approach to the ancient science of the chakras. Her bright energy and clear perspective on this often mystical subject is refreshing and applicable to the modern day woman."

— KINO MACGREGOR, author, founder of Omstars

Cristi brings forth the Ageless Wisdom traditions that allow women to rediscover and liberate the fire within them by embracing the real meanings of the chakra system, mudras, yoga, and other time-tested methods of spiritual liberation. Read this book and release your inner splendor!

—REV MICHAEL BERNARD BECKWITH founder and spiritual director, Agape International Spiritual Center and author of *Life Visioning* and *Spiritual Liberation*

"Cristi takes the reader on a powerful journey of exploring both themselves and the chakras. When you read this book, it feels like Cristi is in the room with you, explaining each detail with enthusiasm and passion. She makes you want to say yes to the journey that is you. Cristi asks that you be an active participant in your learning through rituals and writing prompts, helping the knowledge integrate into your consciousness. This book is a must-have for anyone ready to dive into the mystical world of energy and chakras."

—JILL WINTERSTEEN, founder of Spirit Daughter

"Cristi is a splash of crimson in a world of grey, and her vibrant approach illuminates an ancient practice in a respectful and modern way."

—KATHRYN BUDIG, author of *Aim True* and global yoga teacher

"Calling All Women! Enthusiastic high praise goes to *Chakra Rituals* and its author, Cristi Christensen. This book positively shimmers with embodied feminine wisdom! Cristi lovingly guides us on a journey through the seven energy centers in the body, skillfully weaving practical explorations and sacred illumination. She lives these teachings of wholeness in her own life and knows the process from the inside out. The step-by-step flow is brilliantly organic and easy to follow, with beautiful verses from The Radiance Sutras that inspire wild wonder and awe. Return to this guidebook again and again as your life unfolds, and find deeper meaning each time. Envision this: All women on Earth coming home to their birthright of freedom, power, and joy. Now is the time— our time, your time. This is the love offering, the prayer, the gift of *Chakra Rituals*."

—CAMILLE MAURINE, author of *Meditation Secrets for Women:*
Discovering Your Passion, Pleasure, and Inner Peace

"Cristi Christensen will transform your life. Her work is luminary, practical, and easy to digest for people of all backgrounds. Of all of the chakra books I've ever read, this is the best one. While *Chakra Rituals* is indeed a book for women, I had the gift of reading it from cover to cover, and as a male, I was surprised to see just how much it awakened within me as well. Cristi's voice is a poetic light in these dark times. We are in desperate need to awaken the divine feminine energy on this planet, and I could not think of a better time than now for women to read this book. It's time to wake up to your true authentic power and brilliance, for the benefit of all—Cristi will guide the way."

—JUSTIN MICHAEL WILLIAMS, global speaker and musician, author of *Stay Woke*

"*Chakra Rituals* is equal parts nurturing retreat and adventure into the wild. Cristi Christensen makes what can seem esoteric and illusive completely accessible and actionable...even for a self-proclaimed less-than-wild woman like me."

—ANDREA MARCUM, author of *Close to Om*

"*Chakra Rituals* is the book that we all need right now. In these words, Cristi Christensen enters your home with the attitude of an encouraging best friend. But not just an ordinary best friend. She is a joyful and expansive bringer of radiance and a guide for creativity. *Chakra Rituals* is a magic guidebook for the embodied experience. Don't just read it (now!). Do the practices, say the prayers, contemplate the meditations she offers, use the writing prompts in your journal, and awaken. Oh, and revel in the ecstasy of your own shakti, your own vitality and energy."

—FELICIA TOMASKO, editor in chief, *LA YOGA Magazine*

"What a blessing this book is for women of our time! As women around the world unleash, spread their wings, and transcend all boundaries, Cristi beautifully provides us with the ability to be both wild and grounded, abundant and focused. This book is the perfect guide to help each of us identify the core tenants that can root us in a more meaningful, joyful life, while still allowing us to be free."

—SHELLY TYGIELSKI, author, activist and founder of Pandemic of Love

We are all on a quest for a more vibrant and radiant life, but this journey often lacks a map. Until now. With the wisdom that only ten thousand hours can inform, Cristi unveils the perfect system for accessing our wild nature. This system lives within us: the chakras. Cristi's new book, *Chakra Rituals*, gifts us both the knowledge and actionable practices to unlock our Prana life force, to live a life brimming with vitality and creativity. This book is not just for reading. It is for living!

—JEFF KRANSO CEO and founder of OneCommune and founder of Wanderlust

"My fourth chakra is bursting with joy after exploring my untamed inner wildness, with Cristi's accessible and empowering daily rituals. More than just a heartfelt and riveting read, this book is actually a portal to your truest, most vibrant self."

—ELISE JOAN, Beach Body on Demand super trainer, creator of Barre Blend, and global wellness leader

"With just the right mix of transformative and heartfelt personal stories, powerful Yogic myths, and a step by step guide to help you move through the timeless and potent cycles of the 7 chakras, Cristi ushers you to Do Something! and enter your truest, most evolved and yes, wildest self."

—ANNIE CARPENTER, internationally acclaimed yoga teacher and founder of Smart flow SmartFLOW

"As an advocate for true liberation for all women, I understand that deep and lasting transformation only happens through full integration of the mind, body, and spirit. For many of us, that part is easy to understand, but we struggle with what this looks like in our day-to-day life. What Christensen has so brilliantly done in *Chakra Rituals*, is provide a simple, yet profound guide for how to connect with your chakras and awaken the Wild Woman that is within us all."

—SHELAH MARIE, founder of The Curvy, Curly, Conscious Movement

"Cristi Christensen is one of the best yoga teachers in the world today. In this book Cristi deploys her insights on liberation, aliveness and wholeness to offer women an exciting roadmap for embodying love, confidence and courage."

—SEBASTIAN SIEGEL, writer, director, author

"Cristi Christensen is a force of nature. As a teacher, she ignites powerful joy in her students with fiery, loving energy. Her new book is bursting with her vibrant messages of self healing, women's empowerment and personal transformation. She offers us grounded practices and nourishing rituals with the stunning beauty and elegant style that is classically Cristi. If you are new to studying the Chakra system, Cristi gives you an accessible map and visceral keys to unlock your power, awaken your wild woman and live your life full on!"

—TONI BERGINS, creator of JourneyDance and
Embodied Transformation Method Coaching

"Chakras are an essential part of our well being…creating a balance of mental, physical, and spiritual. Cristi, from her deep organic intelligence, makes you understand the many Chakra layers and helps you activate them with female vigor finding the woman fire within each of us! You will feel reborn with her guidance and live life to the fullest!!"

—ELISABETH HALFPAPP, CoreBarreFit owner and Exhale founding team

"Cristi is an amazing teacher and global trailblazer who has studied, taught and inspired thousands for many years. I love her take on the chakra system and ritual as she guides us through deep healing wisdom in an approachable way; making this ancient framework more available and supportive to us all! Thank you!"

—MILANA SNOW, integrative energy healer and founder of Wellness Official

"Turning the pages of *Chakra Rituals* is like walking side by side with Cristi through her 20-year journey of personal evolution (rooted in masterfully teaching movement and meditation worldwide), where we learn and awaken our potential with each meaningful step. She has created an actionable system for building a life of pure love, deep purpose, complete fulfillment and unbridled joy. Cristi certainly delivers on her promise of giving you the tools to transform your life and create lasting change. *Chakra Rituals* is not a book you will read once and move on from, it is a resource that you will return to for constant inspiration."

—KIRA STOKES, fitness expert, creator of The Stoked Method and
Kira Stokes Fit App

Chakra Rituals

Chakra
Rituals

Awakening the Wild Woman Within

Cristi Christensen

ST. MARTIN'S
ESSENTIALS
NEW YORK

First published in the United States by St. Martin's Essentials, an imprint of St. Martin's Publishing Group

CHAKRA RITUALS. Copyright © 2021 by Cristi Christensen. All rights reserved. Printed in the United States of America. For information, address St. Martin's Publishing Group, 120 Broadway, New York, NY 10271.

www.stmartins.com

Designed by Steven Seighman

Illustrations by Fumi James

Library of Congress Cataloging-in-Publication Data

Names: Christensen, Cristi, author.
Title: Chakra rituals : awakening the wild woman within / Cristi Christensen.
Description: First Edition. | New York : St. Martin's Essentials, 2021. | Includes bibliographical references and index.
Identifiers: LCCN 2020057505 | ISBN 9781250754622 (trade paperback) | ISBN 9781250754639 (ebook)
Subjects: LCSH: Chakras. | Yoga. | Exercise—Miscellanea. | Healing—Miscellanea.
Classification: LCC BF1442.C53 C47 2021 | DDC 294.5/43—dc23
LC record available at https://lccn.loc.gov/2020057505

Our books may be purchased in bulk for promotional, educational, or business use. Please contact your local bookseller or the Macmillan Corporate and Premium Sales Department at 1-800-221-7945, extension 5442, or by email at MacmillanSpecialMarkets@macmillan.com.

First Edition: 2021

10 9 8 7 6 5 4 3 2 1

Contents

The guided practices in *Chakra Rituals* are available as free audio/video downloads at **www.chakrarituals.com**

To my fierce little angel warrior niece,
otherwise known as Queen Caraline. May you
always remember your strength, your bravery,
your wildness, and your true soul beauty.
I love you.

Introduction

"People say that what we're all seeking is a meaning for life.
I don't think that's what we're really seeking. I think that what
we're seeking is . . . the rapture of being alive.*"*

—JOSEPH CAMPBELL

Over my last twenty years of teaching movement, yoga, and meditation in twenty different countries to tens of thousands of women, I have found that most of us are searching for the same things. We want joy. We want passion. We want love. We want confidence. We want power. We want safety, and we want freedom. We want to feel comfortable in our skin and to tap into our essential nature. We want to express our authentic power and to be connected to something greater than ourselves. Ultimately—we want to *become more alive.* But what most women don't know is that there's a perfect system living inside of us, waiting to be unlocked.

This system is your pathway to the full essence of your life. It is your path of integration and of healing, and it will help you live a life *on fire*—grounded in power, love, joy, creation, connection, and purpose.

That System Is the Chakra System

And I'm going to teach you exactly how to activate and unlock the seven chakras in this book.

In today's yoga culture, the chakras have become trendy, sexy, cool, and oh-so-spiritual. I see them every day on T-shirts, jewelry, candles, stickers, and more. By now, most people have heard of the word *chakra* at least once in their lives. But few people know how to use them. Few know how to activate this powerful energetic system for deep transformation.

The chakras are the only system that integrates the physical, mental, emotional, and spiritual body into a single unified map. Unlike classical yoga, which focuses on transcending the body; Buddhism, which emphasizes the heart and spirit; or Western medicine, which only focuses on the body, the chakras integrate all parts of the self. In this book, I'm going to teach you how to use this system, how to activate it, and how to awaken your aliveness through a seven-week journey of empowerment.

Together, we are going on a step-by-step adventure to reclaim our intrinsic wild nature by searching inward—by exploring the caverns of your own *shakti*, your own feminine power, and excavating the precious jewels that are waiting to be placed on your crown. You will awaken inner connections that have been lost. You will reintroduce yourself to your essence and become inspired to stop casting away parts of yourself and your womanhood. Ultimately, my aim is to help you reclaim the inherent *enoughness* that is your birthright.

We will take an ancient science that's often seen as unrelatable and make it applicable to you, the spiritually curious woman, and guide you on a daily self-empowerment journey using the chakras as a road map for transformation.

One of the drawbacks I often find with self-empowerment books is that they keep the teachings in the readers' heads. But real transformation happens through full integration of body, mind, and spirit. It's not enough to just think about transformation: in order for a flame to ignite, we must take action! Which is why the rituals and practices in this book were created—to become the fuel for the deep inner and outer transformation that we've been searching for. The dynamic physicality of this program takes the lessons of the chakras beyond an intellectual point of view and gives you a way to experience them using all your senses. We're taking the chakras out of the mind and into the body and heart in a way that's tangible and fun, so that you can have a lived experience and create lasting change.

Why is this book specifically geared to women? Simply put, the answer is that our time is NOW. There has never been a more important or potent time for women to remember and reclaim who we really are. We were born wild women, yet at some point in time, we forgot. Perhaps our wild nature was cloaked in our conditioning, covered in trauma, or lost in all our responsibilities. Reclaiming your wildness means to return home to your body and to nature, to ignite your sensual prowess, to feel the full flow of your emotions, to rise up in dignity, to come into your power, to lead from your heart, to claim your voice, to tune in to your intuitive gifts, and finally, to take the seat of the queen within yourself. This is the work of the chakra system, and it will serve as our map to restore our wholeness, our wildness, and our aliveness. All women are welcome here! White, black, green, purple, and yellow, all ethnicities, all ages, all religions, anyone who identifies as a woman. This is our time! As we individually do the work to heal and awaken our inner wild woman, we also heal and awaken the collective wild woman—our wild sisters, daughters, mothers, grandmothers, and great grandmothers around the planet.

Chakra Rituals is divided into two parts. I begin each chapter of the book with a sutra from my most beloved text, *The Radiance Sutras*, which is a poetic adaptation of an ancient yogic text—the *Vijnana Bhairava Tantra*, which dates back to AD 800—created by my teacher and mentor Dr. Lorin Roche. To me this sacred text is a living, breathing entity that is an exquisite celebration of all the energies of life. Each verse is an "invitation to wake up to the marvelous symphony within and around us"[1] and is in utter devotion to the divine feminine, or wild woman. Savor them. Let them awaken in you as you read each one line by line, either to yourself or out loud. These sutras set the tone for the magic that's to unfold in the chapter to come. Part I: The Essentials will serve as your foundation, giving you just enough information about the full chakra

system without overwhelming you before we dive into each individual chakra and its practices. These essential first chapters will define necessary terms such as *chakra, tantra, mukti,* and *bhukti* and cover topics such as the subtle and energetic body, where the chakras originated, and how the chakra system works together to bring about transformation. Part I will also serve as your introduction to the power of ritual and the seven empowerment tools and foundational practices we will use throughout the book.

Part II: Daily Rituals for Empowerment will follow a structured step-by-step format for each of the seven individual chakra-focused chapters. Each chapter includes a Radiance Sutra, an introduction to the chakra, the chakra's sacred aspects, anatomy of the chakra, chakra cheat sheet, a story of the goddess, personal narrative, anecdotes, illustrations, and ritual practices that will be central to your empowerment journey.

I know you are busy, so I've created practices that you can modify to fit within your life. Usually, my students must attend trainings or retreats to experience this depth of teaching, but with *Chakra Rituals,* you can practice these empowerment techniques anytime, anywhere. There are even videos and audios of many of the practices (which you can access for free) at ChakraRituals. com.

Everything that I offer comes from the integration of what I've learned teaching over the last twenty years, and embodied through my own teachers, soul study, and deep investigation and devotion to this system. Whether you are an accomplished yogi or just beginning on your spiritual path, you will be able to enjoy the benefits of this book. It's for all of us.

If you are ready to say YES to your wildness, YES to your dreams, and YES to loving yourself and all the magic that this life can be, then let's get started. Let's embark on this journey together! Thank you for allowing me to be your guide. Thank you for allowing me to introduce you to this dynamic healing system that has brought so much depth, power, beauty, and joy into my life. It is an honor I do not take for granted.

Welcome to *Chakra Rituals*!

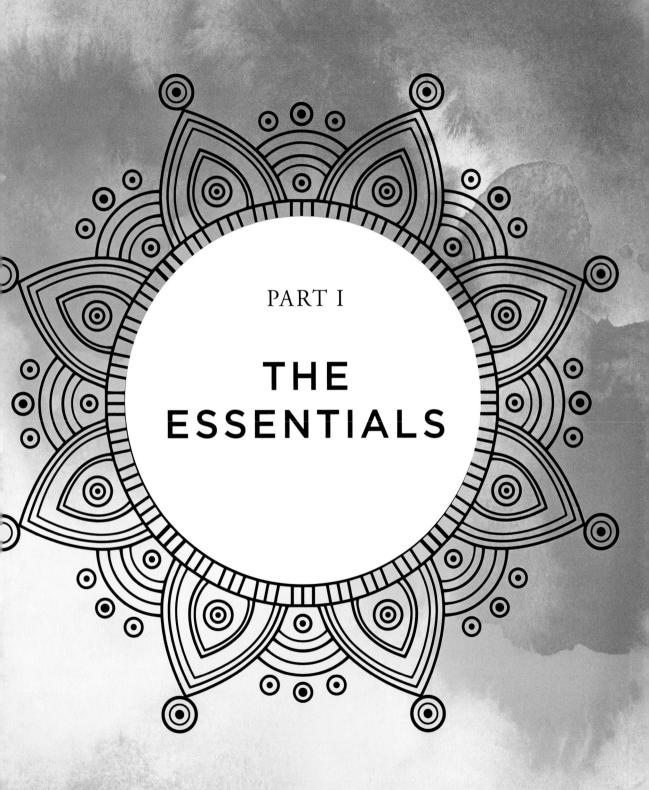

PART I

THE ESSENTIALS

There is a current of love-energy that flows
Between Earth below and Sun above.
The central channel of your spine is the riverbed.
The streaming is as delicate and powerful
As the tingling touch of lovers.
Entering here,
Radiance arches between above and below.
Your whole attention resting in the subtle,
Vibrating in the center of the spinal column,
Tracing this current between Earth and Sun,
Become magnetism relating all the worlds.

—THE RADIANCE SUTRAS: SUTRA 12

1

Chakra Essentials

This is an invitation into the depths of you. Into that which is most sacred, ever loving, and more powerful than any outer force. Buried inside of you are seven radiant jewels of dynamic power and light ready to be excavated. But to access them you are going to need a very special spiritual map. This map is: the chakra system.

Chakra is the Sanskrit word for "wheel," "disc," or "circle"; chakras are often described as wheels of light, whirling vortexes of energy, jewels of intelligence, doorways to the divine, organs of the energy body, and portals to embodiment. The chakras help us:

CONNECT our outer and inner worlds,

HONOR all of who we are and all of what we are made up of—the Earth, Water, Fire, Air, and Space,

AWAKEN our consciousness at seven distinct levels,

KINDLE the fires of transformation, calling us forth into action,

RESTORE our sense of wholeness and our innate wildness, and

ALIGN the wisdom of the earth and the magic and mystery of stars within the sacred core of you.

Classically there are seven main chakras, housed in seven distinct areas of the body.

They run along the spinal column from the base of the pelvis to the crown of the head. It's important to understand that there is no hierarchy amongst them; each one holds its own intelligence, superpower, and expression of life force. This life force energy is known as *pranashakti*. *Prana* is the Sanskrit word for "power," "vitality," "energy," "spirit," or "life force." *Shakti* is the creative, dynamic, wild power and strength of the divine feminine. It is the genius of *pranashakti* that spins, dances, and sings our chakras and our life into motion.

Let's take all of this out of the theoretical and into the experiential. The most direct way to access the power of the chakras is through the body. Wherever you are, take a moment and press down into your feet and feel the ground that you rest upon. Spread your toes and soften your eyes or close them completely. Tune *in* (not out) and notice what you feel. Breathe down into the stability and the strength of the great Mother Earth; feel yourself held in her infinite embrace. Imagine drawing up her wisdom through the soles of your feet, into the channels of your legs, into the base of your pelvis. Place your hands on your low belly now, fingertips lightly touching your pubic bone, and take a single, slow, deep breath in and out. Take your time, do not rush—5 counts in and 5 counts out. As you inhale, feel the breath filling the base of your pelvis from pubic bone to tailbone. As you

exhale, visualize your breath expanding and radiating out from the base of your pelvis like beams of light.

Next, move your hands gently up your low belly to your sacral center, or womb. Breathe in the same way: 5 counts in and 5 counts out. Allow the breath to fill the front, back, sides of your low belly and low back. On the exhale imagine your breath radiating out from your sacral center in all directions.

Continue moving your hands lovingly up the body, placing them on each of the five remaining power centers, taking one slow, deep breath in and out through the center of each one. Refer to the illustration on the next page to help you see where these energy centers radiate from.

- Solar plexus, the space above your navel below the sternum

- Heart, center of your chest

- Throat (hands can gently cup the throat)

- Center of the forehead (hands can be placed front and back of the skull)

- Crown of the head

Just pay attention to what you notice and what you feel. With every breath, you are directing the genius of the life force into each chakra, infusing it with vitality and waking up its intrinsic power and mojo. To finish, ground your feet even more firmly

into the earth and reach your arms up in the direction of the heavens. Don't be afraid to take up more space. Connect into the vastness, the boundlessness above you, to the wisdom of the stars shining down upon you. You are the conduit that connects the earth to the infinite and brings the infinite down to the earth. That is how powerful you are! Take one more deep, slow breath here to strengthen this knowing.

Throughout our journey together, we will explore the chakras systematically, moving through them in ascending order. It's important to remember that even though we will be examining one chakra at a time, they are all connected to and dancing with each other.

And although we are going to dig deep into each chakra, this book is not a chakra encyclopedia—it is a book of empowerment; it's a book to experience, giving you an opportunity to unlock your human potential using the chakras as your map. There is so much complexity and depth to each individual chakra that I literally could have written a separate book on each one. Instead, I've chosen to focus on three to five of the most important elements of each chakra that I know will have the most meaningful impact on your life and best serve to awaken your inner wild woman! So whether you're brand new to the chakra system or you've studied it before, you're bound to learn something new here as the chakras come alive and we experience this dynamic journey together. To give you a sneak peek, this is our pathway of awakening:

FIRST CHAKRA: Muladhara: The earth, the soil, and the darkness, the roots of our origin, the body temple, and embodiment

SECOND CHAKRA: Svadhisthana: The sacred waters that flow, reclaiming pleasure and desire, sovereignty, rites of passage, and sacred sexuality

THIRD CHAKRA: Manipura: The fire that ignites power, will, confidence, unshakeable trust, and healthy anger

FOURTH CHAKRA: Anahata: The breath of life and love in all its forms, the softness and strength of your two hearts, vulnerability, intimacy, and your greatest superpower

FIFTH CHAKRA: Vishuddhi: Vibrating into full expression, communication, authenticity, creative recovery, reclaiming your voice

SIXTH CHAKRA: Ajna: Inner illumination, magic, intuition, honoring the whole of you

SEVENTH CHAKRA: Sahasrara: Opening to the Divine, spiritual power and discernment, gratitude, service, celebration of life

But before we begin our investigation, there are a few more terms we need to define.

THE TWO LEVELS OF EMBODIMENT (OR BODY)

Your body exists on two levels: the *gross* and the *subtle*. The gross level is made up of fat, muscles, bones, blood, fluids—and the five elements Earth, Water, Fire, Air, and Space. You can think of the gross level as the physical body, that which you can lay your hands on and touch, like your hamstring, hand, biceps, breast, or heart. The subtle level refers to the most interior of the body; to that which is most delicate, refined, almost imperceptible. Meaning you can't see, hear, or touch it with your physical senses. We can compare it to air or prana; although we cannot place our hands on it we know it is there and all around us. The chakras exist at the level of the subtle body but impact the gross body directly.

THE TWO CURRENTS OF POWER

There are two vertical currents of power flowing through the chakras: an upward- and a downward-flowing current. The upward-moving current travels up from the earth through the First Chakra to the crown of the head. This is known as the Pathway of *Mukti* ("liberation"). Mukti takes us out of limitation and expands us in the direction of pure potentiality and higher consciousness. Without it we would never grow, evolve, or transform; we would be stuck in the mundane of life. The downward-moving current travels from the sky, the crown, or Seventh Chakra and descends back down into roots of the body. This is known as the Pathway of *Bhukti* ("embodiment," "enjoyment," and "manifestation"). Bhukti makes manifestation possible, giving us the ability to ground our dreams and visions into reality. It also teaches us to enjoy the pleasures of the material world, the gift of our embodiment; to be in a body and to be of this world.

For us to experience the totality of the journey we need both pathways open, free, and flowing.

THREE ENERGETIC PATHWAYS

Within the subtle body there are 72,000 energetic pathways, channels, or rivers of energy. These rivers are what hold and carry the life force to every cell within our body. In Sanskrit these channels are called *nadis,* and for our chakra journey there are three that are important for us to know. They are known as *pingala, ida,* and *sushumna.*

- Pingala nadi: governs the right side of the body and is related to the power of the sun. It is red in color, fiery, and is associated with the qualities of the masculine—logic, doing, linear thinking, to-do lists, etc. In essence it is the energy of action.

- Ida nadi: governs the left side of the body and is related to light and the wisdom of the moon. It is white in color, cooling, and is associated with the qualities of the feminine—intuition, deep listening, nurturance, creativity, spontaneity, etc. In essence, it is the energy of feeling.

- Sushumna nadi: From the root *su*, which means "subtle," and *shumna*, which means "to shine." It is the luminescent central channel that runs through the core of your body from the base of the pelvis to the crown of the head and passes through each of the seven chakras. There are said to be 108 different names in honor of the sushumna nadi. Here are a few of the most common ones you might hear: the Central Channel, the Channel of God, the Path to Enlightenment, the Holy Tube, and the Gracious Channel.

Ida and pingala spiral their way around the sushumna, crisscrossing above and below each chakra until they merge together at the third eye center. You can liken the dance between pingala, ida, and sushumna to a DNA helix and/or to the caduceus, the symbol of modern medicine with its two serpents intertwining. It is from the polarity of opposite energy that the chakras spin. We will explore this deeper in the Sixth Chakra chapter.

SACRED SOUND VIBRATION

Mantra comes from two sanskrit words. *Manas,* which means "mind" or "thought," and *tra,* which means "to protect," or a "tool" or "device." Mantra therefore is a "tool for the mind," or a "tool for thought." Mantra uses sound as a tool to protect the mind and align it back with the heart. The mantra that began all mantras is *om* (or *aum).* Chances are if you have ever taken a yoga class before, you have already experienced the sacred sound vibration of *ommmmmmmmm.* Chances may also be that you might be a little confused about why yogis make this sound and what it even means. *Om* is the primordial sound of creation, it is the "shout of joy that sets the entire universe into motion!"[1] The dictionary definition of *om* is "YES!" It is the universe saying, singing, shouting "YES!" to its ongoing creation, expansion, contraction, and evolution. When we chant *om*, we are harmonizing, aligning our personal *yes* with the *yes* of the universe, saying yes to our prayers, yes to our dreams, and yes to our intentions. Anything we chant after *om* is amplified by the cosmic yes of the universe. In the chapters to come, I will be sharing with you some of my most beloved mantras, and in our Seventh

Chakra chapter, you will even experience a mantra meditation practice.

What you need to know now, however, is that each chakra also has its own sacred vibration or *bija* mantra. *Bija* is the Sanskrit word for "seed." Just as a seed of a flower or a tree holds the full intelligence of all that's to bloom, the seed mantra holds the full intelligence and empowerment of the individual chakra. To unlock and activate its intelligence, the seed needs to be nourished. The way you do this is by speaking or chanting their sacred sounds out loud or quietly within. The seed mantras in ascending order of the chakras are *LAM,* (pronounced "lum") *VAM* ("vum"), *RAM* ("rum"), *YAM* ("yum"), *HAM* ("hum"), and *OM.* You will notice there are only six sounds, as the Seventh Chakra's sound is silence, or in Sanskrit, *shunya*—"exquisite spaciousness." There are also what are called vowel sounds for each of the chakras; in ascending order they are *UH, OO, OH, AH, AI* (pronounced "eye"), *NG,* and *EE.* For your reference, you will find each of these sounds listed in your Chakra Cheat Sheets in each of the chakra chapters as well as in the appendix. I encourage you to play with making all the sounds of the chakras, as each one resonates at its own frequency—speak, sing, and dance with them, and imagine their sound vibrating awake the subtle structures of each chakra and throughout each corresponding region of the body. This is an easy and fun way to invoke and awaken the consciousness that lives within and bring it into full bloom. There are also seed mantras for many of the goddesses, of whom you will learn in the chapters to come.

TANTRA

The chakra system came to us from the ancient yogis of India and dates back over 4,000 years—to the Tantric Period. Before you raise an eyebrow or get hot and bothered, know there is a very good chance you may have a tainted or limited perspective of what tantra actually is and means. To get a full-spectrum definition of what tantra *really* is, let's break down the word. *Tan* means to "stretch," "extend," or "expand," and *tra* means an "instrument," "tool," or "device." This instrument refers to a metaphorical loom, which weaves together different threads of reality, stretching and pulling them in opposite directions to create a new fabric or tapestry. This new fabric integrates that which was separate before— mind/body, spirit/matter, light/shadow, divine/mortal, heaven/earth, masculine/ feminine, sacred/mundane—creating one integrated piece of art. This piece of art is your life. Tantra, and therefore the chakra system, is a tool to expand your life. A life-affirming philosophy that asks you to say YES to life and YES to the world. It honors and celebrates ALL the elements of existence as sacred: mind, body, emotion, breath, soul, individuality, and the infinite.[2] And unlike in classical yoga and the Hindu sects, where spiritual study was reserved only to men, tantra not only welcomes all genders, but reveres *Shakti,* the Divine Feminine, the goddess, aka the wild woman.[3]

THE WILD WOMAN

The wild woman arises to her power by welcoming all of who she is and all of what she feels and longs for. From the nurturing mother to the sexy seductor. From the conqueror to the sweet friend. From the fierce businesswoman to the spiritually sassy. Throughout history, women have been put in boxes by our families, societies, or cultures, impressing on them the "proper way" to behave. These boxes and systems are outdated. Women are not just one thing, nor should we try to be. Clarissa Pinkola Estés, bestselling author of *Women Who Run with the Wolves,* says the wild woman is a dying breed, an endangered species, as we have been cut out from our innate, instinctual nature. The work of reclaiming our wild woman is intrinsically tied to the awakening of each chakra and its elemental energies. Together, we will claim our womanhood and stop suppressing, ignoring, or denying any aspect of ourselves as we begin to welcome, celebrate, and love all of who we are as unique and powerful women. It is time to call back the disintegrated parts of yourself and honor and own your deepest desires and listen to the wisdom singing within. You are a force of nature; it's time you own it!

The Seven Longings and Welcomings of The Wild Woman

	7 longings	7 welcomings
	I long to feel at home in the universe, to let my light shine and **know** I am aligned with the Divine.	I welcome the Queen, the High Priestess, the peacemaker. I welcome knowledge and freedom, expansiveness and peacefulness.
	I long to **see** beyond the veils of illusion, to see through the eyes of beauty and love. To discern and see what is really going on.	I welcome the seer, the sage, the sorcerer, the inner wise woman, the magician, the intuitive, the dreamer, and the visioneer.
	I long to **speak** and express my truth. To say what I feel and to be heard.	I welcome the artist, the dancer, the writer, the singer, the speaker, and poet. I welcome authentic expression, the power of my voice, and the potency of my words.
	I long to **love** and to be loved, to hold and to be held.	I welcome the lover, the healer, the wife, the mother, the daughter, and the friend. I welcome romance, love, and devotion.
	I long to feel my personal **power**; to know I AM worthy and know I AM enough.	I welcome the rebel, the warrior, the fierce businesswoman, the boss lady, and the bitch. I welcome independence, autonomy, energy, and success.
	I long to feel sensual **pleasure**, the spark of aliveness and the tingle in all my secret places. I long to celebrate the gift of my embodiment.	I welcome the virgin, the sexy seductor, the slut, and the Empress. I welcome the dance of desire and the flow of my emotions.
	I long to be grounded, rooted, connected to my body, and to be held by the earth. I long to feel at **home**.	I welcome the instinctual, the primal, the raw, and the wild. I welcome the nurturing mother, the fool, and the adventurer.

Ultimately what I want you to know is that you CAN have it all. You can be the powerful CEO and the vulnerable lover. You can have material success and spiritual connection. You can have an open heart and healthy boundaries. This is the path to true embodied liberation. This is the path to wild feminine freedom. With your spiritual road map now in hand, let's journey on and learn about the power of ritual.

Worship does not mean offering flowers.
It means offering your heart
To the vast mystery
Of the Universe.
It means letting your heart pulse
With the life of the universe,
Without thought and without reservation.
It means to be in love.

—THE RADIANCE SUTRAS: INSIGHT VERSE 147

2

Ritual Essentials

Chakra Rituals is not a book to just read or contemplate—it is a book to *experience*. We do this through the practice of ritual.

Rituals, just like the chakras, serve as a bridge connecting our outer and inner worlds. A ritual is anything in which we offer our heart. They give us the freedom to take responsibility for the direction and purpose of our lives and help us recognize the meaning and magic around us, things so easily obscured in today's world.

Rituals help us . . .

REMEMBER who we are and what we are connected to through repetition, and they are performed with . . .

INTENTION. Thus, their outcome is

TRANSFORMATIVE. By practicing them, we gain a better

UNDERSTANDING of ourselves, and **AWAKEN** our authentic power. Most of all, they activate

LOVE, the most powerful energy there is.

You can think of this entire seven-week journey as one momentous ritual made up of smaller rites, which are the individual acts within a ritual. I will refer to these rites as empowerment tools or ritual practices. In each chapter, we will explore these practices in seven different ways: altar building, mudra, breath practices, body prayers, meditation, embodiment, and writing contemplation.

Let's take a closer look at each of the empowerment tools.

1. I was first introduced to the art of altar making by one of my first teachers, Shiva Rea. Before the opening of any of her workshops or retreats she would take the time to build altars both large and small around the yoga room as a way of creating sacred space. Each altar was uniquely and intentionally designed to inspire, support, and anchor our practice in the divine. Filled with fresh flowers, candles, colorful fabrics, incense, and statues of different deities, each altar vibrated beauty and devotion. This is one of the many yogic practices I have fallen in love with and taken out of the yoga studio and into my home.

As your first ritual practice each week, you will create an altar in your own home. Now perhaps prior to now, your only construct of an altar or the idea of one comes from the church and might hold religious connotations. The practice we are doing together is not religious and doesn't conflict with any religious or spiritual beliefs. I want you to think of building an altar not as a religious act, but as a way of creating personal sacred space within your home—full of what *you* believe in and what *you* love. Your altar creations are a way to align, celebrate, and honor all that lives in your heart and all that you want to embody. If that includes Mother Mary, Durga, Archangel Gabriel, or any other goddess or god, your children, or family, by all means feel free to include them. There are no rules; you can do no wrong. Throughout the chapters, I will offer suggestions based upon the energetic qualities of each chakra and things that I use in my own altar creations. If you

don't resonate with something, don't use it. If you don't have an item on the list, don't worry. The intention of altar-making isn't to turn this into an intense shopping list. Look around your home and see what you can find. You can place your altar in a window sill, on a bedside table, on top of a dresser, or even on the floor (see the photos on the previous page for examples). They will become a visual, living manifestation of the energy of each chakra. They will reflect back to you what is already inside of you. The mere sight of your altar will serve as a blessing to heal, inspire, and attune your energy to the divine. Your altar space will be where you will return to each day to perform your daily ritual practices.

2. **Mudra** The word *mudra* means "gesture," "seal," or "finger posture." And although you might not be familiar with the word, I guarantee you've been using mudras more than you might think. Think about the gesture you make when you see someone you know from far away. Or when you congratulate someone on a job well done. Have you ever thrown up a peace sign? Or think about the last time you got cut off in traffic and another spontaneous hand gesture occurred! These hand gestures are mudras—and they emphasize and accent our experience of life.

The word comes from *mud* which means "delight" or "pleasure" and *dru* which means "to draw forth."

Your hands are some of the most powerful instruments that you possess for healing. If you've ever been on the giving or receiving end of a massage, a reiki treatment, or any energy healing modality, you know what I'm talking about. The power of touch, coupled with intentionality and consciousness, has a profound ability to awaken, heal, and balance our physical and energetic bodies. You can think of the subtle practice of mudras as the yoga of your hands. Just like we can bend our bodies in all different shapes, creating beautiful asanas to elicit a certain response in our bodies, we can do the same thing with the connections we make with our fingers and our hands.

3. **Breath Practices/Pranayama**
Pranayama is the yogic word for "breathing techniques." Prana is the life force energy that emanates through all living things. *Pra* means "to fill" and *na* means "to live." *Ayama* means "the extension or the expansion of." Therefore practicing pranayama techniques gives us the opportunity to extend and expand our relationship with our own energy and the energy of life.

My teacher Camille Maurine so beautifully explains that breathing is a reciprocal relationship between your body and the larger body of life, nature, and the cosmos. It is through this relationship, this dance of giving and receiving, that we commune with and give back to life and life is given to us. Every time you inhale, you breathe in oxygen, spirit, vitality, and sacred life force energy, but from where? From the heavens, from the cosmos, from all of nature, the trees, and all growing things. Every time you exhale you give the gift of life back through the release of carbon dioxide which feeds the whole of nature, from the forest to the seas. By acknowledging this relationship, you recognize yourself as intrinsically interlocked with all of life; you are one with the larger whole of the universe.

Throughout *Chakra Rituals* you will explore a variety of breathing techniques that will amplify this relationship between you, the great mystery of life, and all of the chakra energies.

4. **Body Prayers** We cannot go on a journey of empowerment, embodiment, or awakening aliveness without getting off our *asana* and onto our mats! Movement is the medicine that will strengthen your physical form, move the stagnation and heaviness out of your body, and connect you to that which is most sacred—your body.

Body prayers are short and simple, flowing breath-based vinyasa yoga practices that are dynamic, fun, chakra activating, and healing. Vinyasa means "to move or to place in a special or conscious way," just as in the placement

or arrangement of musical notes in a song. Each chakra has its own special body prayer which you will learn. When you move and breathe with intentionality and awareness, you connect to something greater. It is from that place that prayer naturally arises from within and you become devotion in motion. Included in each chapter are beautiful step-by-step photographs of the postures along with simple written instructions. You also have access to free online video content at www.chakrarituals.com where I will guide you through each of the prayers. The sequences are safe for all levels and all body types. Please take care of yourself and do the best you can and know you always have full permission to modify the practices to fit your body and needs.

5. **Meditation** Being a yogini and on the spiritual path, meditation was something I thought I should be doing and thought I should be good at. The problem was, I wasn't. I found it boring. When I managed to stay awake, I struggled to sit still and not look at the clock every ten seconds. The more I tried to stop my mind from thinking the faster it would race. All this changed when I met my mentor and teacher Dr. Lorin Roche. Lorin is one of the world's leading meditation teachers, who along with his wife, Camille Maurine, is revolutionizing the way we think of meditation and the way in which we meditate. Together they have authored

seven books, taught all over the world, and created their own style of meditation called Instinctive Meditation. I met Lorin back in 2007 when I was running Exhale Center for Sacred Movement in Venice, California. One day he walked into my office and asked me if I meditated. I paused for a moment, not sure how to answer, and then said, "Yeah, sure . . . well, not really, but I try." He then asked me how I meditated. I looked at him like, huh? As far as I knew there was only one way to meditate. So I quickly sat down cross-legged on my office floor, closed my eyes, and held my body as straight and tall as I could to show him I knew how to meditate. No more than five seconds had passed when he told me to get up and said, "Cristi, in all the time that I've known you, I have never seen you be still for one moment of one day, so why would you think you need to be still in your meditation?" Before I could respond he added: "The reason you don't enjoy your meditation is because you are doing *someone else's* meditation!" He suggested that the next time I meditate, instead of fighting against my natural impulse and desire to move, rock, or sway, that I give into it fully and completely. Just when I thought my mind couldn't be blown any more he said, "You don't even have to sit down, you can even dance!"

One of the biggest lessons here is there is no one-size-fits-all approach

to meditation; that is why in *Chakra Rituals* you will have the opportunity to experience many different meditations—from guided visualizations, to touching, to sounding and singing, to shaking, and even growing roots like a tree (more on that later).

6. **Embodiment** There seems to be a lot of confusion in the spiritual world around the importance of the physical body. Many traditions claim the body is "the root of all evil" and that the only way to experience true liberation or freedom is to transcend it along with all of earthly reality. I don't know about you, but I do not want to waste my time on earth trying to transcend my humanness or ignore the fact that I am here and in a body. I want to celebrate the gift of embodiment. I want to celebrate spirit descending down into this womanly form and access the integrated intelligence that is living in my bones. The yogis believe that everything that has ever happened to us is stored in the cellular memory of our tissues. We know things in our bones to be true. Even if our minds forget, our bodies remember. Embodiment—to me—is the true definition of yoga. It is the coming together, the sacred union of mind, body, heart, and spirit. The embodiment rituals in this book will support the awakening of the intelligence of each chakra that is already living inside of you and bring you home to your body.

7. **Writing Contemplation** Writing contemplation and journaling have been a part of my daily life for the last twenty years. I think of my pen as my magic wand, and my journal as a place where my intuitive wisdom and guidance speak to me. The page is a safe place to process, purge, express, and unapologetically be me—a source of inspiration, creativity, and where I can reflect, release, and speak my unedited truth. Over the course of our time together you will be keeping a journal. I will offer daily questions relevant to each chakra. This will deepen your connection to yourself and the energy of the chakra. The invitation here is to be authentic, raw, and real. Your words are between you and the page. Try to resist the urge to censor or edit yourself, fix your grammar, or even your spelling. Just write!

It is not required, but I suggest you go old school and take pen to paper, even go out and buy yourself a beautiful book to write in. Why write by hand? It forces you to slow down and take a break from your technology. Studies have also shown that writing by hand cultivates your wisdom, sparks your creativity, and puts your mind in a state similar to meditation![1]

FOUNDATIONAL RITUAL PRACTICES

There are a few foundational practices you need to know before we get started. Please take your time to experience each of the foundational practices below. We'll be using them often throughout our ritual practices. If you forget, don't worry, you can always refer back to these pages to review. Some of our ritual practices, like altar building and embodiment, do not have a foundational practice, so you will experience those for the first time in our First Chakra chapter.

FOUNDATIONAL MUDRA EXERCISES

You can think of the energy practice of mudras as subtle body training. Recall from chapter 1 that *subtle* means that which is most delicate or refined, meaning it may take a little time and practice to build and heighten your sensitivity. Just know the more you play, the more active the energy will become. Once you begin to tune in to this energetic circuitry, you can start experiencing the immense power that lives within your fingers and palms. Be patient and curious. One of the simplest ways to do this is by supercharging your hands.

Here are two supercharging exercises for you to play with. You may do them seated or standing.

Mudra Warmup 1:
Fire Kindling

1. Place the palms of your hands together and start to rub them vigorously—keep rubbing your hands until they get hot. You can liken this techique to rubbing two sticks together to kindle a fire.

2. Once you've built up a good amount of heat, release the hands onto your lap with palms facing skyward.

3. Soften your eyes or close them. Simply start to pay attention to any of the subtle changes or sensations you feel. This may be in the form of a tingling, buzzing, or throbbing sensation, a change in temperature, a feeling of density or lightness, or you may even see a color.

4. If you feel or see nothing, do not worry! It's totally normal. You are just beginning to wake up the subtle energy and build your sensitivity here. Stay for another breath or two. Then blink the eyes open.

Mudra Warmup 2:
Open the Hand Chakras

I first learned this exercise from Anodea Judith, author, therapist, and one of the great wisdom keepers of the chakra system. It is designed to open up the energy channels in the palms of the hands known as the *hasta* or hand chakras. Yes, we have dynamic wheels of energy in our hands too!

1. Extend both arms out in front of you at shoulder height.

2. Turn your right palm face up and your left palm face down.

3. Close your hands making two tight fists, squeeze, and then re-extend the fingers all the way.

4. Begin to close and open the hands rapidly, really extending the fingers each time. *Repeat 10 times.*

5. After the tenth one, turn the left palm up and right palm down, and repeat 10 more times.

6. Turn the palms to face each other and separate them just a few inches.

7. Soften the eyes or close them and one last time notice, pulse, play with what you feel. Picture, sense, imagine, feel the chakras in your hands opening, these dynamic wheels of light spinning. You may experience a magnetic pull to bring the hands closer together, or you may play with taking the hands as wide apart as you can, while still feeling the vibratory effect. Play with the sensations you feel. If you don't feel anything, just go ahead and charge the hands up one more time.

I recommend that you do at least one of these exercises each week before you do your mudra practice.

FOUNDATIONAL BREATH

Many of our breath, meditation, and mudra practices will begin with a technique I call the *nourishing breath*. It is a quick and easy way to energetically clean the slate, oxygenate every cell of your body with fresh prana, and ground you into presence. The focus is on inhaling a full 360-degree breath into the torso—filling the low belly and low back, the front, sides, and the back of the rib cage, and the front and back of the heart. When we breathe this way we access 65 percent more of our lung capacity and revitalize and nourish the whole of the energetic body.

1. Come to a comfortable seated position. Ground down through your pelvis and rise up tall through your spine.

2. Let the hands rest on your thighs.

3. Exhale once completely, and then begin inhaling deeply through the nose, filling the whole of the torso **front** and **back** with your breath; low belly, low back, rib cage, and chest for the count of 4.

4. Pause, feel the fullness of the 360-degree expanse for the count of 2. *Be sure not to strain.*

5. Open your mouth and exhale out for the count of 4 releasing the breath completely.

6. Begin again. Inhale, your breath fills and expands the belly, low back, rib cage, and heart 360 degrees, nourishing the whole of you.

7. Pause for the count of 2.

8. This time exhale out with an audible sigh to the count of 4 getting empty, empty, empty.

9. Continue on your own for 5–10 more rounds. Inhale 360 degrees for the count of 4, hold count of 2, exhale count of 4.

You can also listen to the how-to audio at www.chakrarituals.com

Notes

If this technique is new for you, begin by focusing on breathing only into the back of the body. And then use the power of the exhales as a sweet release. This will ensure that the whole energetic body is nourished as the chakras open to the front and back of the body.

FOUNDATIONAL BODY PRAYER

Move through this foundational sequence 1–3 times on each side, paying close attention to your breath and the transitions back up to the top of the mat. Take your time to embody this sequence as it serves as the foundation for all others to come.

1. Start standing, feet hip-width apart, hands in prayer at your heart

2. Inhale, reach your arms up overhead

3. Exhale, hinge from your hips and fold forward. (Bend your knees if you need to.) Inhale, lift chest to a flat back

4. Exhale, step your left foot back, and bend your front leg 90 degrees. Low lunge

5. Inhale, step back to high plank

6. Exhale, knees down, hug elbows into the body, tone your belly, and lower yourself to the ground

7. Inhale, rise into baby cobra

8. Exhale, push back to downward-facing dog

9. Step to the top of the mat

10. Inhale to elongate the spine. Exhale, fold forward

11. Inhale, slowly roll up to standing

12. Exhale, hands return to prayer

Repeat sequence on the second side stepping back with the right leg.

FOUNDATIONAL MEDITATION: GROUNDING CORD

To truly be wild and free you must have strong, deep, stable roots: something to ground into so that you have a solid base of support to root, rise, and expand into freedom. Without this grounding anchor, "you risk floating aimlessly, being battered by the winds and the waves of life."[2]

This meditation technique will connect the center of you to the center of the earth. It will give you the necessary stability and support to rise up in the direction of spirit and release down into the support of earth—rising in strength, presence, truth, and releasing anything that doesn't serve you now.

1. Come to a comfortable seated position. Let the palms rest on your knees or thighs. Soften your eyes or close them completely.

2. Start to wiggle your hips from side to side to locate your two sitz bones.

3. Once you find them, press down into them and rise up tall through your spine.

4. Take 3 deep *nourishing breaths.*

5. Next, bring your attention to the base of your pelvis and call forth your powers of imagination.

6. Visualize the trunk of your favorite tree growing down from the base of your spine. The trunk extends down

through the ground and grows down, down, through all the molten layers and textures of the earth until it reaches the fiery core of the mother.

7. Breathe deeply in and out as you feel yourself tethered, held, and grounded into the support of the earth. This energetic connection creates what is called a grounding cord.

8. Your *grounding cord* also acts as a release valve to let out any excess energies you hold in the form of tension, stress, worry, or fear.

9. With every exhale is an opportunity to release what no longer serves you down your grounding cord.

10. Shift your attention to your inhales and begin to drink in the exact nourishment that your body needs today. Like a tree, receive this energy up through your stable roots of support.

11. Sit with this visualization for 3 more deep breaths. Know you are steady, know you are strong, know you are always tethered to this great body!

You can also listen to the how-to audio at www.chakrarituals.com

Another powerful way to explore this practice is standing up, grounding through your two legs and two feet.

In the upcoming chapters, I will refer to

this practice by instructing you to "drop a grounding cord."

Writing contemplation

1. What do the words *Wild* and *Woman* mean to you and invoke in you? Do they excite you or frighten you?

2. Do you consider yourself a wild woman? Explain.

3. What are the ways in which you suppress your wild feminine power?

HOW TO USE THIS BOOK

Chakra Rituals is designed to be a step-by-step, week-by-week journey through the seven chakras. Each week, you will activate a new chakra through the reading and the daily yoga-centric ritual practices—not with the goal of making you a chakra expert, but to give you a lived, embodied experience of each chakra, along with practices you can come back to again and again. As you work your way through the book, know there will be some practices that you will love and others that you may resist doing completely. This is totally normal. Meet your resistance but show up anyway, remain open, and do your best. For your first time working through the book, I highly recommend

you commit to moving through the book in seven weeks, one chakra per week, as it was intended, but of course I recognize life gets busy sometimes and that's not always possible. So if needed, you can move at a slower pace that works for your life, whether that be fourteen weeks or seven months. Our days will be broken down as follows:

DAY 1: Read the chakra chapter + set up your altar + writing contemplation

DAY 2: Mudra practice + writing contemplation

DAY 3: Breath practice + writing contemplation

DAY 4: Body prayer + writing contemplation

DAY 5: Meditation + writing contemplation

DAY 6: Embodiment + writing contemplation

DAY 7: Integration: this is the part of life most of us skip, but it is the most important—pause to reflect and integrate the new lessons with the greater whole of our experience. It's also the perfect time to return back to any of the previous days' readings or rituals.

If you go through this entire program and commit to the ritual practices, your life will change. And most important, you will rebuild the most sacred and important connection there is—your connection to self. Ready to awaken the wild woman within? Let's begin!

PART II

DAILY RITUALS FOR EMPOWERMENT

Follow the path of the life force
As she flashes upward like lightning
Through your body.
Attend simultaneously
To the perineum, that bright place
Between the legs,
To the crown of the skull,
And to that shining star-place
Above the head.
Notice this living current
Becoming ever more subtle as she rises,
Radiant as the morning sun,
Until she streams outward from the top of the head
Into all-embracing gratitude.
Thus become intimate with the life of all beings.

—THE RADIANCE SUTRAS: SUTRA 5

3

Coming Home to the Root of You

THE FIRST CHAKRA

Our journey into true empowerment and embodiment begins in the dark, fertile soil of the earth, the sacred element of our First Chakra, Muladhara. *Mula* means "root," "origin," or "beginnings," and *dhara* means "foundation." This is the root foundation in which your energetic body and every chakra is built upon; it must be strong, stable, able to hold all the energy that we are.

The First Chakra asks you to get down and dirty, to investigate the soil and the tendrils of support that your physical body and life are growing in. These are the roots of your origin, your body, your belonging, and your connection to the great Mother Earth. The roots of your aliveness, your fears, your survival, and your wildness. Each root feeds you with a different kind of nutrient, security, and strength. As they are tended to, they become healthy and strong and can grow deep and wide. They will hold you steady, even when the ground below you shakes, which at times it most certainly will. You will remain anchored, unwavering in your foundation, and connected to the root of you.

From this solid foundation, you will be able to rise up in the direction of liberation and freedom and manifest your dreams on the physical plane. The First Chakra asks you to explore your humanness, what it means to be at *home*, in a body, in the real world, rooted to this earth; able not only to survive, but to thrive.

ANATOMY OF THE ROOT CHAKRA

According to Vedic and tantric philosophy, each chakra has what is called a *yantra*. A yantra is a visual tool composed of ancient geometrical shapes or patterns. Each shape is steeped in symbolic meaning. We can use this tool to help unlock and better understand the energy and wisdom of each chakra. By looking at the visual form, even meditating on it, we can connect with the yantra's wisdom and activate it in our own body.

The symbol for the Root Chakra represents stability, strength, and endurance; the sacred feminine and masculine; and the journey we must travel to both liberate and awaken the raw power within. This symbol is a red lotus flower with four petals. Red is the color of shakti, pure aliveness, birth, and blood. Four is the number of structure and solidity. The four petals are oriented in the four cardinal directions (N, S, E, W) and represent the elements (Earth, Fire, Air, Water) and the dimensions (Vertical, Horizontal, Before, and Beyond). Inside the lotus is the most stable of all geometric shapes—the square. The square stands as the steady ground upon which we build our foundation. Inside the square is a downward-pointing triangle which symbolizes the dynamic, creative, feminine force known as shakti, or the pathway of embodiment. Inside the triangle is a symbol of the masculine—the shiva lingam—which resembles an erect phallus and represents

the pathway of liberation and freedom. Wrapped around the lingam three-and-a-half times is the serpentine goddess known as Kundalini. Her spiritual energy rests dormant at the base of the pelvis and is the wild, raw, shakti power. When she is aroused, she moves upward, piercing each chakra one by one. Just as the yantra depicts, the aroused Kundalini has the potential to awaken your own raw power and the energy of each chakra. But to do so, we must begin at the base of your body—the Muladhara.

SACRED ELEMENT OF EARTH

The Earth element is associated with the Root Chakra. This is the power of the darkness. The deep restoration of midnight, the remembrance that all things begin in the dark. Here in the soil of the First Chakra we plant a seed, and when it is nurtured, nourished, and watered, the seed sprouts roots that grow down and out, and then it pushes up, up, up, to the light. Out of the darkness, light and life are born. In time, life will wither and die and be returned to the earth to be decomposed, composted, and fed to the soil. That is the cyclical nature of the earth. The earth brings us back in contact with the wisdom of our elders and our ancestors that runs through our blood and is in our bones. The power of the earth is asking you to reclaim the holiness of your body temple, to heal your body, and to open your eyes to see the great goddess you are!

YOUR CHAKRA CHEAT SHEET

Name	Muladhara Mula (Root) Dhara (Foundation, Support)	**Bija Sound**	LAM (pronounced LUM)
Meaning	The Root in Which All Things Grow	**Vowel Sound**	UH
Physical Location	Base of the Spine: Perineum	**Energetics**	Groundedness, Safety, Stability, Security
Element	Earth	**Affirmations**	I am safe. I am secure. I am at home in my body. I love my body. I belong here. The earth supports and nourishes me. Rooted to the earth I cannot fall.
Color	Red		
Sense	Smell		

Body parts related	That which is most dense: the teeth, the bones, specifically the spine, base of the spine, the legs, the ankles, and feet The immune system
Effects of Deficiency	Disconnected from the body, scattered, easily swept off feet, accident prone, caught in the mind, fearful, anxious, light body, inability to sit still, poor boundaries
Effects of Excess	Heavy body both physically and energetically Stuck, stagnate, overly strong boundaries Lethargic, depressed Material fixation Inability to let go—holding on too tightly
Balance	Vital health and wellness Feeling safe, secure, and grounded Able to take care of oneself, make money, and manifest dreams into reality Intense desire to LIVE! Feeling at home in one's body, comfortable in own skin Presence in the here and now Able to let go and relax

HOME

Earlier, I mentioned the significance of home to the Muladhara. What does home feel like to you? When you think of the word *home*, what visuals and sensations come over you? How would you like to feel at home? Safe, secure, warm, comfortable, loving, steady, fed? Is it a place where you can let go, rest, and relax? Think, perhaps, on your ideal home and the one in your memory, with connection and comfort on the one hand and contention and struggle possibly on the other. Now, you might be imagining home as the actual structure in which you lay your head at night, but let's expand the walls of this mental image to include home as your beautiful body temple, home as your mother and family, and home as a child of the interconnected earth. Safe, secure, stable, loving, beautiful. Now, don't all these words still apply to how you want to feel at home—in your skin and on this planet? Let's take a look at each connection's foundation and examine the soil in which we have buried our roots.

1. Body Temple

Before we go any further, I want to share a little story with you about a Sanskrit mantra that changed my relationship with my home. Sanskrit is the ancient language of the yogis, and a mantra is a verbal tool that connects the mind to the heart. I remember the first time I heard the words sung, "*mama mana mandire, mama mana mandire*." I had no idea what they meant, but they sounded like the most beautiful words I had ever heard. As I began to sing along, I was taken over by emotion and tears began to well up in my eyes. I was touched so deeply, yet still (at least on the intellectual level) did not know what the words meant. But on a deeper, embodied level, I did. I continued to chant/sing the mantra *mama mana mandire, mama mana mandire* for years. I would often fall asleep and wake up repeating it, still not "knowing" what it meant. Until one day when I met a man named Guarvani, a *kirtan* (devotional) singer who was giving an intimate workshop at the yoga studio I ran. To my surprise, he began to sing the mantra and then paused to tell us a story about its meaning. The prayer I had been chanting for all those years was, in English, "My body is a temple, my body is a sacred place!"

Most of us don't treat our bodies as sacred, let alone a temple. As a survivor of abuse, which by the age of ten began to include self-harm, my body was more like a war zone than a sacred anything. I went through years of over-training, lack of food, and cyclical binging and purging. I cursed the size of my legs, my muscles, and my breasts as they started to form. My worth, my perceived beauty, and my ability to make the Olympic gymnastics and diving team were tied to the number on the scale and my body fat percentage. This was further perpetuated by my coaches and my mother, who was terrified of getting fat herself. As a young girl, my sister and I would joke that our mom was having air again for dinner. My gymnastics coach would pinch my forehead and say, "You should not be able to pinch more than that anywhere on your body." Food was not nourishment, but something that I had labeled either good or bad. If I ate something on the bad list, I would punish myself either by purging; doing an obscene number of jumping jacks, sit-ups, or push-ups in my room; or not eating the next day.

Even though the decades of abuse had ended by the first time I heard the words *mama mana mandire*, the deeper healing my body craved was just beginning. New neural pathways needed to be created in order for me to see and relate to my body in a whole new way. Chanting the mantra was nourishing the soil my root relationship with my body was growing in and opening up a new pathway *home* to my body.

Being embodied is about feeling at *home* in your own skin, connected to your physical form, sense of self, and the world at large. It is the recognition of the sublime power, primal instincts, and embedded wisdom that this body holds. Sadly, much of the world is cut off from

these inherent gifts, as we live in a society that frequently honors the mind and its mental capabilities above the body and its physical truths. We spend most of our time living in our heads, caught between fear and fantasy, the past and the future, disconnected from the present and our wants, needs, and desires.

The tantric perspective from which the chakra system is derived offers a different perspective: "Nothing exists that is not divine." Hence *the body is the temple.* This earthly reality of relationships, responsibility, emotions, and feelings is not what limits us but instead is the foundation for our embodiment, each a doorway into coming more fully alive. This philosophy has the potential to heal the schism between the body and mind, matter and spirit, earth and heaven as it embraces and honors the whole. What could be more spiritual than being fully human, fully awake, and fully alive?

Say it with me: *My body and mind are a temple. My body and mind are a sacred place.* I amended the translation of the mantra slightly to celebrate the alchemical weaving of body, mind, heart, and spirit. The daily ritual practices at the end of this chapter will guide you back into this knowing and train your awareness on returning home and feeling your physical form. I promise you will reclaim the *aliveness* that pervades your entire body and vibrates throughout!

My Body Prayer

An empowered, wild woman knows that beauty comes in ALL forms. The most beautiful and powerful thing is a woman grounded in her own body, secure, and owning her whole self. You may know a woman just like this—you know because when she appears, you cannot take your eyes off her. Her strength and power can be felt even from across the room. This woman honors and respects the temple her wild goddess resides in.

Can you believe that the author of this book—the same girl who used to stand in front of the mirror every day and pick herself to pieces—now looks in the mirror and absolutely loves and celebrates her body? I am in utter amazement of all the things my body can do, the energy, the strength that it has. Daily, as part of a ritual, I thank my body. I touch my own skin, run my hands over all my curves ever so tenderly and lovingly, and I thank it for not quitting or abandoning me, even with all the years I rejected, abused, and almost killed it. I apologize, and I ask for forgiveness of every cell, organ, and tissue. There are days this practice still brings me to tears, as I cannot believe I did not see the gift of this body before. It is time for you to enter a state of fuller love and appreciation for all your body does for you, no matter its current condition. Through self-acceptance you heal. By honoring yourself, you can change the relationship you have with your body. This is the first step.

This is my body blessing; use it as an inspiration to create your own.

Oh Great Mother!
I love you
As you love me
Thank you for creating me so beautifully.
This body is amazing!
Bless my feet so that I may feel your ground
of support with every step I take.
Bless my legs rooted in strength and stability.
May they allow me to walk my own true path.
Bless my swinging hips and bountiful booty
that I get to shake wild and free.
Bless my womb, where life itself is created and
where I receive pleasure just for pleasure's
sake.
Bless my belly and the power that resides
inside me.
Bless my breasts, small yet beautiful and bra-free.
Bless my heart that it may never tire of
loving, healing, or forgiving me.
Bless my throat for I may sing my own
authentic song.
Bless my ears that I may hear and be heard.
Bless my lips that I may smile and snarl.
Bless my eyes that I may see the beauty and
the magic that is me and surrounds me.
Bless every inch of this womanly temple that
is imperfectly perfect for me.

Remember: your body is sacred. All of you is sacred. The divine rests at the altar of your heart, inside the temple of YOU.

2. The Mother Root

Remember, *mula* means "root," and the root from which we all grow is our mother's womb. She is our first home and our primary root relationship. In the womb, the fetus literally roots itself into the mother's uterine wall, and the umbilical cord then fuses mother to child. We can imagine it as our first tendril of support, our survival lifeline that feeds, nourishes, and connects us to our mother. While in the womb, we feel everything our mothers feel. We experience every stress, fear, and hormone that is released. If she felt safe, secure, and loved during her pregnancy, so did we. When we are born, we are helpless and unable to see, so we sense our mother/caregiver by the smell (the sense related to the First Chakra) of her skin. She (or he or they) is the one who cares for our physical survival needs of food, water, shelter, and safety, along with our emotional survival needs of interconnection, love, and affection. It is through this primary relationship that we learn a basic sense of trust, decide if the world is a safe place, and establish an instinctual sense of belonging.

Childhood is an extremely impactful time in the formation of the Muladhara Chakra, so digging around in the soil where your root foundation was laid might shed profound insights on who you are today. Do you know what your birth mother's pregnancy was like? Were you expected, planned, or a surprise? Was your father or your mother's partner in the picture? If so, were they a supportive, stable, grounding force? Our ancestors live on in our DNA, that of our mother, grandmothers, and great grandmothers, as do their tribal memories, and traumas remain imprinted within the subtle body. Science is beginning to show that there is DNA present in the mother's womb going back three generations![1] And on a more somber note, other studies are showing that intergenerational trauma goes back as far as seven generations.[2] In other words, we are more physically connected to and impacted by our lineage and bloodlines than we once thought. It is our work to take responsibility for our own lives and tend to the tangled system of initial root connections within our family to heal these wounds of our origin, the traumas of our bloodlines, in order to feel whole, grounded, secure, and loved.

A huge step in my own healing came when I took the responsibility of mother to the little girl inside of me. To some extent we are all victims of less than perfect beginnings and parenting. So we all have to learn to give to ourselves what for whatever reason our mothers/

caregivers were not capable of giving. What are the ways in which you can lovingly tend to the little girl inside of you with sensitivity and vigilance? How can you make her feel safe and certain that you will not abandon her? Tell her you are so sorry for whatever she has had to endure, and assure her you are here and will protect, care for, see, and love her wildly no matter what. Our survival literally depends on the care of the mother. Take on this role within you and give yourself what you need.

Mothering yourself is understanding what you need and giving it to yourself. This extends to how you nourish yourself through food, how you tend to your body via movement, and how you pamper, rest, and replenish yourself. *What are some of the ways you can deeply nourish yourself on a daily basis?*

3. Home in the arms of the Mother Earth

Our journey home would be incomplete without taking into consideration this blue marble of a home in which we all belong. Mother Earth IS our home. She holds our wisdom. She constitutes all that we are—the Earth, Water, Fire, Air, and Space. She is the grounding force that we tap into to fill our bodies up with the vitality of aliveness that only she can provide. Through her we ground our excess charge that often manifests as fear, worry, or stress, that keeps us disconnected from our bodies and overtaxes our nervous systems. When we let down into her, releasing what we do not need, we are able to rest, recalibrate, and restore. She nurtures us, cares for us, and provides us with the stability and shelter we need for our lives. She teaches us patience, as she is never in a rush. The more we root down into her, the safer, lighter, and freer we will actually feel. I have found profound healing can come from connecting to the great love of Mother Earth. Her reliable embrace never tires of nourishing us and can help us heal the wounds we may have from our own mothers.

FEAR AND ITS ANTIDOTE: MEET MOTHER GODDESS KALI, THE ORIGINAL WILD WOMAN

Fear is one of the ruling emotions of the First Chakra. It is one of our most powerful, primal, and natural emotions. We all have fear; it is not a mistake. It is what keeps us alive, but it also often keeps us from fully living. Fear can be the paralyzing, shadowy force that stops us in our tracks. It can halt us in our trust of others, ourselves, and the flow of life. It pushes on the chest, preventing us from taking a deep breath. It disconnects us from our spirit, from our guidance, from the earth, and from our power. Today we call upon the most ferocious, wild, untamable form of the great Shakti in the Hindu pantheon, Mother Kali, to help us confront our fear and change it to empowerment. You don't have to be Hindu or religious to appreciate Kali. Contrary to popular belief, honoring the gods and goddesses of this tradition is not about worshipping something external. Think of them as archetypes within, used purely as a reflection, reminding us of our own power.

Kali is not your typical goddess, or what you might imagine when you first hear the word *goddess*. Her name means "the black one," or "that which devours everything," as she is both creation and destruction. She is the dark goddess of the earth, the fertile soil,

WAYS TO CONNECT WITH MOTHER EARTH

Mother Earth, however important to our health and well-being, has grown distant from our thoughts and polluted from our societies' excess. We have forgotten we are her children; we have forgotten that we belong to each other. The easiest and fastest way to build or renew your connection with Mother Earth is to get outside. Take refuge in nature and in the natural world, and try the suggestions below:

- Go out in nature: hike, bike, walk, lean up against a tree, listen to the sounds of nature.
- Watch the sunrise or sunset.
- Rest in earth savasana: lie belly down to the ground.
- Walk barefoot on the grass, sand, clay, or rock.
- Sing and dance to the earth.
- Garden: get your hands in the dirt; plant a tree.
- Bring earth into your home with a plant, tree, or herb bed.

the womb, the darkness of midnight. She is the divine protector who, at the surface, appears utterly terrifying, but as we take a closer look at her symbols and iconography, we find that she is the most exquisite source of love and freedom.

She is depicted in many ways and in many forms. In this chapter's illustration, you are seeing the modern wild woman version of Kali that portrays her fierce essence. But I also want to talk to you about one of the classical depictions of Kali, to give you the full range of her power. In classical interpretations, Kali is often depicted with four arms, reminiscent of the four petals of the shakti lotus. In one of her four hands, Kali holds abhaya mudra, which instills protection and peace and dispels fear. Through this gesture she is saying, *Fear not, I will protect you.* Kali teaches us that we are never without fear. The goal is not to become fearless, but to be able to stand in the face of fear, to even bless it, to know that you are protected and can release, rise, and transform through anything.

In another hand Kali wields a sword, which she uses to sever the attachments that no longer serve us. It is her sword that can free us from our limited beliefs—from the situations and relationships that make us feel small, from work that no longer fulfills, and from our own complacency that keeps us stuck and lulls our wild woman back to

sleep. Think, *where in your life do you need Kali's sword to cleave you from your disabling attachments?*

In her third hand, Kali classically performs varada mudra, the gesture of offering boons and blessings. It is also a symbol of the great compassion and love she offers as we undergo this transformational awakening.

In the fourth hand, she holds a severed head, symbolizing the release from our own afflicted mind/ego. She saves us from the inner negative thoughts, doubt, and shame that can destroy us.

Her hair is disheveled and dreadlocked, her body naked (symbolizing the authentic self), and her tongue hangs out, reminding us of all the tastes, flavors, and textures of life. She is not here to conform to or please others; she is only concerned with helping you confront what makes you most afraid and what is keeping you from realizing your greatest potential. She is the original wild woman! Her colors represent the full cycle of existence: red (life force energy, passion, and Root Chakra), white (bones, death, ending), and black (Earth, soil, darkness of the womb).

Reflect on something in your life, maybe a fear that is stopping you from feeling your power or keeping you from what you really want. As you acknowledge your fear, call to Kali, "Oh great mother, I invoke you in this space to take away my pain and fill me with your grace." Imagine Kali standing before you. Offer your fear to her. There's no right. There's no wrong. You can offer your sorrow, your pain, your joy, your ecstasy. You can ask her to be gentle as she helps release and liberate you from all that binds. In exchange for your fear, Kali offers you a great blessing, perhaps in the form of a word, mudra, or symbol. As you receive this blessing, you can repeat her seed mantra

klim (pronounced "kleeeeem There are many mantras for her more gentle form.[3]

My hope is that, now tha classic form of Kali mixed w of our wild woman Kali depicted in this book, you can feel the full range of her power, the Divine Goddess from which transformation springs forth and into which everything is absorbed.

THE PRACTICES: 7 DAYS OF GROUNDING

Day One: Altar

Your Earth Altar is the place you will come to every day for your grounding rituals. As you build your altar, remember that the ideas below are just suggestions based on things I use in my personal practice. Your altar should represent your unique foundation. Anytime you feel lost or disconnected, the mere sight of your altar will serve as an anchor to tether you back to the strength of your foundation and welcome you home.

Earth Altar Essentials

- Something red (cloth, candle, stone)
- The element of Earth (twigs, acorns, leaves, flowers, soil, anything you find in nature)
- An item that symbolizes stability for you

Earth Altar Inspirations

- Photos of your ancestors, your family, places in nature you feel a deep connection to
- Fruits of the earth: apple, pear, cinnamon stick
- Shape: square

- Money (a manifestation of the material world)
- Your *sankalpa* statement (see Writing Contemplation, page 44) written on a piece of paper
- Crystals: garnet, hematite, black tourmaline
- Oils: vetiver, black spruce, cassia
- Tarot Cards: The Fool, The Empress, Ace of Earth, Ten of Earth

Refer to the Quick Charts in the Appendix for extended meanings of crystals, oils, and tarot cards.

Writing Contemplation

1. In yoga we have a beautiful initiating word, *sankalpa*. *Sankalpa* translates to "intention," "wish," "aim," or "prayer." Here at the start of your journey, what is your intention? What prayer are you making to yourself? What is your aim or hope right now? Can you distill it down to a few words, a phrase, or a sentence? Now imagine your sankalpa as a seed and plant it into the metaphorical fertile soil. Every day, return to this statement as an act of nourishing the ground of support from which your highest resolve will blossom.

2. Tend to your "physical" root needs. These are the roots of your health, work, finances, food, and physical home in which you live. Honestly examine each of these and dig around and see what needs to be nourished, tended to, or cared for more deeply. How can you take responsibility to strengthen your foundation and create a solid structure to thrive in each area of your life?

3. Our very first initiation into this human reality is birth. Take some time and write about the story of how you incarnated on planet Earth. Ina May Gaskin, one of the most famous midwives in the world, wrote, "Our birth story matters. It matters because it is the way we all begin our lives outside the source, our mother's bodies." If you do not know the story of your birth, interview your parents, guardians, or older siblings if possible to help you put the pieces of the story together.

Day Two: Mudra—Bhumisparsha

The mudra we are practicing today is called bhumisparsha mudra. *Bhumi* means "earth," and *sparsha* means "to touch." This mudra brings you back in touch with the great ground of support of Mother Earth, reminding you that you are never alone and are always held by the larger body of the earth. All you have to do is anchor your roots down into the soil to receive her nourishing embrace, wisdom, and medicine. Practice this mudra anytime you feel lost, fragmented, or disconnected from your grounded sense of self as it will tether you back home.

Here are the step-by-step instructions:

1. Find a comfortable seat in front of your altar. Sit up tall, ground into your pelvis, and drop a grounding cord (see page 26 if you need a refresher).

2. Supercharge your hands (see page 22 if you need a refresher).

3. Take your left hand to your heart and place your right over your left.

4. Take one deep, slow, rich breath in and out as you welcome yourself home to your body and home to your heart.

5. Release your right hand down and lightly touch the earth.

6. Gently extend all five fingers and imagine tendrils of support growing down from each of your fingertips into the earth.

7. Soften your eyes, soften your body, and take ten slow, deep, *nourishing breaths*. Breathe into your roots of support and into your connection with the Great Mother.

8. With every inhale, allow her reliable, healing, grounding energy medicine to fill your body. With each exhale, allow yourself to rest more deeply into her embrace. Know you are safe, supported, and loved.

9. Imagine now your heartbeat syncing with the heartbeat of Mother Earth. Sense all of her wisdom and love being merged into the power of your heart, reawakening your knowing that she too is your Home.

10. When you are ready, open your eyes, release the gesture. Take a few moments to pause and witness how you feel. Bow down and give thanks to Mother Earth.

You can also listen to the how-to audio at www.chakrarituals.com.

Writing contemplation

1. What is your relationship to Mother Earth, nature, and the natural world? How do you treat her? What is one thing you can start to do to honor her more deeply and build upon this connection?

2. As a way of connecting to and building a relationship to Mother Earth and Nature, finish these sentences:
Mother Earth allows me to _____
_____.
Mother Earth is teaching me _____
_____.
When I spend time in nature _____
_____.
Nature speaks to me with _____
_____.

3. Where do you feel at home in nature? What is an easy way that you can begin to spend more time here and with Mother Earth?

Day Three: Breath—Breath of Descent

When we disconnect from our body, our roots literally lift themselves up out of the ground and our energy darts upward to escape into the mind, trapping us in fear, anxiety, worry, or fantasy. This causes a split between the mind and the body. The pranayama technique we are exploring for the First Chakra consciously works to redirect your energy back down into your body, into your roots of support that bring you in contact with the ground, your legs, and feet. I call it the Breath of Descent as it follows the downward flow of movement or energy, known as *apana vayu*. It serves your ability to eliminate physical (urine, stool, menstruation, carbon dioxide) and energetic (fear, worry, anxiety) waste from the body. This creates a feeling of safety, stability, and strength inside of you, while signaling to the nervous system it is okay to relax, to let go, and to release.

Let's give it a try. Here are the step-by-step instructions:

1. Find a comfortable, grounded seat. Rest your hands, palms facing down, on your legs, and drop a grounding cord. This will immediately connect you to both the earth and your physical form.

2. Close your eyes or soften the gaze steady on a point and take one deep *nourishing breath*.

3. Inhale deeply through your nose for the count of 3, drawing your breath down into your low belly, low back, pelvis, pelvic floor, into the pulsating wheel of ruby red light of your Root Chakra.

4. Exhale your breath out through your hips, legs, calves, ankles, and down into the soles of the feet for the count of 6. Your breath won't actually go down this far, but your energy will.

5. Inhale down into your low belly, low back, tailbone, and pubic bone for the count of 3. Exhale down and out through the channels of the legs and feet for the count of 6. Pay attention to the subtle vibrations of pranic energy building in your legs and especially in the soles of the feet.

6. Continue on your own for 5 to 7 more breaths. With each inhale, feel your breath and energy descending back down into the temple of your body. And with each exhale, soften a little bit more and follow the flow of gravity to release into the support of the earth.

You can also listen to the how-to audio at www.chakrarituals.com.

Writing contemplation

1. As we continue to expand our definition of *home*, where do you feel most at home? And with whom do you feel most at home?

2. What pulls your attention from really being here? What distractions do you turn to so you don't have to be present in this moment? Social media, TV, food, alcohol, sex, drugs? What are you resisting feeling in your physical body, in this moment in time? How is this distraction helping you to cope or heal? Is it bringing you closer to or further away from what you really want?

3. Now that you have looked at the roots of your physical needs, let's tend to your nonphysical (primal) needs: such as a feeling of safety, belonging, grounded-ness, and companionship. What are some of the things you need to feel safe, grounded, and supported?

Day Four: Muladhara Body Prayer

The more you plug into the earth, the more it brings you down into your flesh and into your body. This is why the practice of yoga is so helpful with grounding. Your body prayer for the Root Chakra will move at a slow yet steady pace. Focus on your breathing and your foundation (everything that is touching the earth) in every pose. This sequence will work to strengthen and stretch the channels of the legs and hips, and will fortify your connection to the ground you stand upon. Please take care of yourself and do the best you can, and know you always have full permission to modify the practices to fit your body and needs.

Suggested use: Repeat the sequence 1 to 3 times on each side. Follow the pictures to come or watch the how-to video at www.chakrarituals.com.

Start standing, feet hip-width apart, arms by your sides, palms facing forward.

1. Inhale; bend knees, lift hands to waist height. Exhale; turn palms down and powerfully press your arms and legs straight. Repeat 3 times

2. Turn feet out 45 degrees. Inhale; hands to chest. Exhale; squat. Push out through your palms to extend your arms. Repeat 7 times

3. Inhale; reach your arms up overhead. Exhale; sit down into yogic squat, malasana. Inhale

4. Exhale; turn feet parallel, straighten legs, and fold forward

5. Step your left leg back, tap your left knee down. Inhale; low lunge

6. Exhale; shift your hips back and straighten your front leg. Inhale; rebend your front knee returning to low lunge. Repeat poses 5 and 6 three more times

7. Come to table pose. Exhale; round spine: cat pose

8. Inhale; extend the spine: cow pose. Move between cat and cow pose, steps 7–8 three more times

9. Exhale; push back to downward-facing dog. Hold for 5 breaths

10. Step to the top of the mat

11. Inhale; slowly roll up to standing

12. Exhale; hands to prayer at your heart

Be sure to repeat on the second side stepping back with the right leg. That constitutes one round.

Writing contemplation

1. What was your experience with the First Chakra body prayer? How did it feel moving your body in this way? How did you feel in your body? Strong, stable, tight, open, anxious? Were you able to meet yourself where you were at today?

2. What is your current relationship with your body? Do you love it, honor it, nourish it? Or do you punish it, abuse it, ignore it? How has your relationship with your body changed over the years?

3. What are three things you can do today to support your body?

Day Five: Meditation—Healing the Roots of Your Origin

Healing the roots of your origin is a creative visualization that honors your beginnings. When we tend to our ancestral roots, we strengthen who we are. We have the opportunity to find our place on the earth, to recognize our place in the line of our ancestry, to grow healthier, stronger roots, and to live a truly empowered life.

In this meditation, you will metaphorically be calling forth your birth mother and father. If you have never met your biological parents and do not know their names, you are welcome to honor the caregivers who raised you. If you are estranged from either or both of your parents, this meditation can be incredibly healing. Do your best to remain open and be with whatever arises.

1. Come into a comfortable seated posture. Press down into your sitz bones, rise tall through your spine, and imagine your ruby red grounding cord growing down deep into the fiery core center of the earth.

2. Close your eyes and take three deep *nourishing breaths*, in through your nose and out through your mouth.

3. In your mind's eye, call forth your mother and your father. Ask them to come and be present with you now.

4. See your parents standing before you. Your mother on the left and your father on the right. It does not matter what your relationship has been with them up to this point, or if it's been years since you have seen them, or even if they are still on the earth plane or not. Picture, sense, imagine, feel your parents standing before you.

5. Stay grounded in you as you witness their presence. Look to just your father and repeat his full name three times. Look him in the eye, thank him for coming, for answering your call, and for giving you life. Breathe deeply, releasing any fear or anxiety down through your ruby red grounding cord of support. Be with everything you feel.

6. Turn to your mother now, look her in the eyes, and repeat her full maiden name three times. Thank her for coming, for answering your call, and for giving you life. Breathe deeply, releasing any fear or anxiety down through your grounding cord. Breathe.

7. If there is anything else you would like to say to either of your parents, take a few moments to do so. Anything you want to express, ask, or request of them, do this now. Remain open to any and all healing taking place in this moment however small or large; keep releasing down through your grounding cord and breathing deeply.

8. Now see yourself before you. Look into your own eyes. Repeat your full name three times beginning with "I AM [name]." Claim the person that you are with your full presence. See yourself taking up more space, claiming your place in this world while honoring where you came from. Rise in your full strength, power, and radiance. Visualize your roots growing down, deep and wide, your branches, flowers, and fruits extending up and out into the heavens.

In the power and the presence of "I AM [name]," claim who you are, where you came from, and your right to be here on planet Earth.

9. Sit as long as you want to, then take your pen to paper and write about your experience.

You can also listen to the how-to audio at www.chakrarituals.com.

Writing Contemplation

1. Family forms our first foundation. What is your current relationship with your family, birth mother, or your caregivers who raised you? Do you feel like you belong to that family, or are there things that need to be mended or healed within these primary root relationships?

2. What patterns and behaviors did you inherit from your ancestors? How can you begin to heal and/or celebrate them?

3. Self-care is not a luxury, but a necessity not only to survive, but thrive. Make a list of at least three self-care rituals that you can incorporate into your daily and weekly life.

Day Six: Embodiment—Abhyanga

Embodiment at the root level is about returning home to your body through physical, tactile, nourishing touch. The practice of *abhyanga*, or warm oil self-massage, brings you back into loving contact with your flesh and bones while nourishing your tissues, muscles, and skin. This is an important step toward self-love and acceptance. It is also deeply soothing for the nervous system, almost like you are putting a protective layer or coating around each and every nerve ending, allowing the whole body to relax.

Additional benefits include:

- Improves circulation; lubricates joints, bones, and internal organs
- Boosts your health and immunity
- Activates your "happy hormone," oxytocin, giving you an uplift of joy and deeper bonding to yourself
- Anti-aging; hydrates and softens skin

You will want to do this practice in a warm, private place, where you will feel totally comfortable and won't be distracted. I also suggest you designate one towel as your abhyanga towel, as it will get a little oily.

1. Select an organic oil. I recommend sesame, coconut, or sunflower oil.
2. Warm ½ cup of oil on the stove for a few minutes. You want it warm, not hot. If you do not have access to a stove or want to skip this step, you may warm the oil up by rubbing it between your palms.
3. Take a small amount of oil in your hands and begin gently, yet firmly, massaging your flesh. I always begin with my belly, making nice big circles; initiating loving contact and acceptance with my womb.
4. Move next to the breasts, circling the tissue in both directions several times.
5. From there move to the neck, the shoulders, and start to make your way down the arms, wrists, palms, and each finger, infusing positivity, care, and love with every stroke.
6. Move to the back body: low back, mid back, kidneys, and buttocks.
7. Continue to your hips and make your way down the legs to the ankles and the feet. Explore circular motions around the joints and long up-and-down strokes on your extremities. Pay a little extra attention to the soles of the feet, as there are many nerve endings and *marma* (energy) points in the feet. They are also how we make contact with the ground.
8. As you continue to massage your body, feel the healing touch of your

hands honoring every bump, curve, bone, wrinkle, and scar. Solidify the remembrance that this body is a temple and a sacred space.

9. Once your whole body is saturated in oil, let it stay on for 5 to 15 minutes. Don't skip this step. This gives the oil a chance to penetrate deeper into the tissues. This is the perfect time to do a few rounds of the *Breath of Descent,* to repeat your body blessing, or, if you have a little more time, draw a bath.

10. Thank your body for all that it did today, how it carried you, and how it strengthened you. Tap into the awe and appreciation for its resilience and its ever-changing beauty. Saturate yourself with gratitude for this body that is yours.

11. Jump into the shower and rinse the remaining oil off your body or make it doubly luxurious and soak in the bath!

Try this practice 2 to 3 times a week and see how you begin to love the skin you're in!

Writing contemplation

1. How did you feel after your first self-love massage? What did it feel like to touch your own skin, your own body in this way? Were you able to sense and feel yourself really in your body? Notice any sore muscles or tender spots? Or any spots you found a new appreciation for?

2. Create your own body blessing. Remember mine? *Thank you, Mother, for I am beautifully and wonderfully made.* This body is amazing! Start with your feet and make your way up the whole body. Reclaim the joy of being in this human form.

3. Kali provides the invitation to liberate and transform our fears into blessings. What's holding you back? What are you most afraid of? And how is this keeping you from living? Can you take a closer look at your fear? What is underneath it? Can you trace it back to where it originated? Consider what might happen if this fear came true—what is the worst thing that could happen? Can you offer this fear to Kali to be transformed?

- Your body and mind are a temple.
- Tend to and honor the roots of your origin.
- Self-care is not a luxury, but a survival need.
- Mother Earth is your HOME.
- Offer the fears that bind you and keep you playing small to Mother Kali.
- Kali is the original Wild Woman!

In the First Chakra, we started to change the lens of perception through which we saw our own bodies. Using compassion, tenderness, and self-love we created a body blessing, upped our self-care game, and honored our survival needs, which created a safe, strong, and sacred environment for us to come home to. Now that this foundation is set, we can dive deeper into taking ownership of "our own sweet place" and truly experience the power, the magic, and the pleasure that this womanly body brings.

Today is your day of reflection and rest. Take some time to reflect upon your most important takeaway from this chakra chapter. If there was only one thing you could remember from this chapter, what would it be? Maybe take a moment to note it down as we continue the journey, that one thing that you want to remember. Now is also the perfect opportunity to return to any of the previous days' exercises or readings.

Consider all the pain and all the pleasure
you have ever experienced
As waves on a very deep ocean which you are.
From the depths, witness those waves,
Rolling along so bravely, always changing,
Beautiful in their self-sustaining power.
Marvel that once, you identified with
Only the surface of this ocean.
Now embrace waves, depths, undersea mountains,
Out to the farthest shore.

—The Radiance Sutras: Insight Verse 136

4

Your Own Sweet Place

THE SECOND CHAKRA

Once the seeds of our intentions are planted in the earth, we need water to help them grow, which brings us to the Second Chakra—the Svadhisthana Chakra, related to the element of water. *Sva* means "self," *svadha* means "sweetness," and *adhista* is "where your being is established." It represents a private, special place inside of each woman—the womb, sexuality, sensuality, and the things that bring about pleasure.

As a woman you are designed, programmed even, to be a dynamic, sensual, pleasure-filled being. Your woman's body is meant to be enjoyed, or as I like to say, INjoyed. This is your sacred birthright. But at some point, whether through society,

religion, family, or friends, something happened that may have shut you down to that which is most natural: your body, your hunger for pleasure and desire, the flow of your emotions, and your sacred sexuality. Maybe it was shut down due to guilt, shame, or how others responded to your sexual choice or orientation, or physical, emotional, or sexual trauma, something way too many women are faced with today. Nothing freezes the sacred waters faster than trauma or abuse, as it cripples the life force, stops the flow of movement, and numbs the bodily sensations.

This chapter comes with a gentle warning, as we will be entering into realms of the deeply personal, even the taboo, which may push some of you out of your comfort zone. I invite you to continue anyway, asking yourself this question: "How long do I want to wait to come alive?" I promise to hold and guide you lovingly as we meet, name, and explore the entire sacral region and tenderly behold the energy it bears. We will look at rites of passage, sacred sexuality, and work to break the dams we have built that block our emotions from flowing. I guarantee this work, along with the ritual practices, will help you come back in touch and in tune with your feminine nature, so you can taste the sweetness of Svadhisthana.

ANATOMY OF THE WATER CHAKRA

Recall our discussion of the First Chakra: its core symbol is a square. Being the most stable of all geometric shapes, the square gives us the strength of solid structure and foundation. As we move from the First Chakra and stability to our current chakra on flow, our core shape is now a circle. A circle is less stable but more free and fluid. The circle represents the feminine, the continual flow of life, and the cyclical nature of it. The circle connects us to the fullness of the moon, the ruling celestial body of Svadhisthana.

The moon impacts the tides and the sacred waters that flow internally and externally, making water the element of Svadhisthana. Its color is depicted as vibrant orange. It blends red (the color of the Root Chakra and the feminine as seen in our menstruation) and yellow (the color of our next chakra, fire, and power).

Within the circle, we find a silver crescent moon, representing the different phases of the moon and the different faces of the ever-changing woman. The silver color speaks to the *soma* or nectar that pours forth from the light of the moon, nourishing and restoring us. This color also represents the reproductive fluids. You may imagine Lakshmi, the goddess of abundance and love, seated on the center of the six-petaled lotus of your Second Chakra.

SACRED WATERS

We all intuitively have a special connection with water. Perhaps it is because we are born out of embryonic fluid, spending our first nine months floating in the waters of creation in our mother's womb. Water is feminine, flowing, and feeling. It is flexible, adaptable, ever changing in its form: evaporating into steam, freezing into a block of ice, or taking the shape of earth as it follows the path of least resistance. Its nature is movement, and as it moves it creates, sustains, and supports all life. Think of all the movements of water: waves curl, then crash; rivers rush with rapids; tide pools whirl and swirl; waterfalls cascade; lakes, ponds, and pools circulate. Ruled by the moon, water is always changing, just like us. Water teaches us we can be contradictory: soft and fierce; gentle and tumultuous; able to glide, float, and be gently carried. Water teaches us that we have the power to turn boulders into sand.

Our nature is like water. On the physical level, 60 to 70 percent of our bodies are made up of water. Water fills our cells, our blood; lubricates and protects our joints, discs, and brain. It flushes waste out of our bodies, allows us to cry, starts the process of digestion via saliva, and regulates body temperature through sweating.[1] Our bodies require the flow of movement, just like water, to function and sustain health. What happens when water is not circulating, not moving? Bacteria and algae form. Mosquitoes lay eggs, and stench accumulates. Without movement, water turns from life-giving to disease-ridden. Something similar happens in our bodies when our waters are not flowing. Stagnation settles into the tissues, rigidity manifests as pain in the joints and muscles, emotions freeze up, and the creative life force is blocked.

YOUR CHAKRA CHEAT SHEET

Name	Svadhisthana
Meaning	Your own sweet place To stand in one's own place The Abode of the Goddess
Physical Location	Sacral center (low belly between navel and pubic bone)
Element	Water
Color	Orange
Sense	Taste

Bija Sound	VAM (pronounced "vum")
Vowel Sound	OO
Energetics	Emotions, sensations, desire, sexuality
Affirmations	I FEEL. I feel connected to my feminine power and to the flow of life. I allow my body to be suffused with pleasure. I welcome pleasure into my life. I welcome the flow of desire. I honor the flow of my emotions. I am in touch and in tune with my sexual power.

Body parts related	Hips, sacrum, low belly, low back, sexual organs, inner thighs, knees (how we move), large intestine—absorbs water back into the body, hydration, bladder, kidneys, urinary tract, entire reproductive system: womb, ovaries, fallopian tubes, testicles, genitals, and all reproductive fluids
Deficiency	Rigid in body or mind; lack of movement; dry, emotionally numb, insensitive, sexually frigid, non-orgasmic; loss of connection to the feminine and feminine power, loss of appetite for life; lack of desire, passion, and pleasure; creatively stuck, stagnant; fear of change
Excess	Sexual addiction, sexual manipulation, sexually acting out, emotional dependency; overly sensitive, ruled by emotions; mood disorders, poor boundaries, too much movement; lost connection with the sacred part of sexuality Seeking larger and larger experiences like jumping out of a plane, taking crazy risks, sexually acting out in an attempt **to feel** something. This could lead to overindulgence and addictions related to food, sex, alcohol, and drugs.
Balance	Emotional intelligence; juicy, sweet, fertile, sacred sexuality; ability to go with the flow; fluid, graceful movements; life is colorful, vibrant, meaningful, and pleasurable.

MEETING YOUR OWN SWEET PLACE

I have never liked the word *vagina*. It's cold, clinical, lifeless, and it carries no juice or passion! It is neither sexy nor empowering and, from my perspective, adds to the disconnection and lack of seeing this area of the body as sacred. There is a Taoist saying that the beginning of wisdom is to call things by their correct name. It was not until I learned the word *yoni* and its multilayered meaning that I knew I had found the correct name to refer to this area of my body.

Yoni is a Sanskrit word that translates to "womb," "origin," or "creative cauldron." More than just the "vagina," the yoni encompasses the entire female reproductive system and therefore the whole body region that the Second Chakra governs. In the Sanskrit language, in order to understand the innermost meaning of a word, you can examine each individual letter on its own. I learned a powerful and "secret" teaching about the yoni through this letter-by-letter process that transformed my relationship with everything down under. Rufus Camphausen literally spells it out in his stunning book *The Yoni: Sacred Symbol of Female Creative Power*[2]:

Y= the animating principle, the heart, the true self, union
O= preservation, brightness
N= moon cycle, fertility, motherhood, lotus, nakedness, pearl
I= love, desire, pain, sorrow, to shine, soma

This holistic definition exudes greater symbolism, depth, feeling, and flow than the word "vagina." While that word brings to mind a taboo section of a Western medical textbook, Camphausen's *yoni* summons ideas of the divine feminine like "union," "brightness," "motherhood," "love," and shakti.[2] It speaks to the spiritual journey, emotional range, the true meaning of yoga, union, and the many initiation cycles of a woman's life. Instead of signifying only a label for our sex organ, *yoni* offers an integrated understanding of the power, potency, and sacredness of a woman's body and the Second Chakra's intelligence. Even if you do not relate to the word yet, try on the definition. Take your hands to your yoni, your womb, and reread the definition. Take your time and breathe deeply into each word. See how it makes you feel and how it connects you softly with your feminine power.

LIKE A VIRGIN

We all know the famous Madonna song lyric. We all remember the awkwardness, the uncomfortableness of *our* first time. But what if I told you that we got it all wrong—that the original meaning of the word *virgin* had nothing to do with sex?! It was a term used to describe a sovereign woman, a woman who was not married, owned, or possessed by a man. In this sense, virgins are women who are free, independent, wild, and willful—all aspects of the divine feminine. The Second Chakra teaches us that the collective healing of women's bodies and psyches requires us to reclaim our virginity.

You may ask, "How the hell am I going to do that?" What you will NOT have to do is run out and get a divorce, become celibate, or exorcise all the partners of your past! Instead, becoming virgin is an act of reclaiming *ownership* over one's self and one's body by tenderly working to re-inhabit it. For a myriad of reasons, ranging from physical trauma, major surgeries to the yoni, childbirth, breastfeeding, outdated cultural or religious beliefs, and/or sexual trauma, some women have never felt they were the authority over their own body, or that their body even belonged to them. To stand in one's own place—one of the translations of the Svadhisthana—requires you to remember that your body belongs to YOU! Not to a man, woman, coach, boss, parent, or a child that you gave birth to, or a child that you're nursing.

Your body belongs to you and only you! This reclamation is essential for any woman whose sexual or emotional boundaries were violated, ownership was stripped, and virginity in this sense was robbed, as it gives a woman her power back. It is equally important for any woman who has abused and neglected her own self, and let's face it: virtually all of us have done this.

Becoming a virgin again means becoming the empowered wild woman. When you take ownership over what is rightfully yours and re-inhabit your body through the practices outlined in this chapter, healing blossoms, self-love deepens, sensation returns, and healthy boundaries grow. Through consistent practice, the power and pleasure of your body and its aliveness can be restored.

RITES OF PASSAGE

Once you have become virgin again and have unlocked the wisdom of the yoni, a comfort with and connection to your sacral center and your own skin happens almost automatically. Now, through this new lens of understanding and embodiment, we can more easily navigate and honor the four rites of passage, three of which are unique to women, and all of which involve the yoni and the Second Chakra. The rites of passage are milestones in our actualization as wild women, and while not every woman will experience each rite or even in the same order, each one is a threshold in the journey of self that deserves its own sacredness.

Moving in the chronological order many women experience these rites, our journey into womanhood begins with getting our moon cycle, starting that process of becoming a woman. As we sexually mature, the second rite is having sex for the first

WAYS TO CONNECT WITH WATER

- Relax in a body of water (ocean, lake, pool, river, bathtub, shower).

- Feel the water soothe you and lift you as it flows around your body, washing away any tensions or negativity, caressing your skin and hair. How does the water feel on your skin? How does it feel when you move your body through it?

- Listen to the sounds of water— waves crashing, waterfalls, rain, music that is flowing.

- Drink more water.

- Move like water: in wavelike patterns; fluid and flowing, rock your pelvis forward and back, circle your hips and shoulders, unhinge your jaw, and let the whole body sway.

time, and the third is the period of fertility and giving birth, figuratively or literally, to a child, business, album, book, or any creative project. And the fourth rite is moving into menopause and becoming the crone, or the wise woman, with the cessation of the menstrual cycle. Now you may not personally relate to all of these rites now or ever in this way, whether because of your age, the rite you are in, or if you are in the percentage of women who will never menstruate for various reasons. The most important takeaway is that regardless of whether you bleed or don't, there is an acknowledgment of each initiation into your own phases of womanhood. When we reflect on these rites, we have the opportunity to look into how we really feel about our own moments in time and our transitions to come. We are given a chance in the present day to honor and heal anything that needs to be and to restore the lotus of the Second Chakra. Not all of us will encounter each of these rites of passage—and does that make you or me any less of a woman? Absolutely not! Wherever you are in your journey of womanhood, that space is sacred. For me, this healing came through the examination of my first rite of passage.

When I was just shy of fourteen, I was a gymnast with dreams of one day going to the Olympics. Getting my period was something that meant my career was over, that my body was changing, that I had too much body fat and would not be able to jump, twist, flip high enough. Back in the early 90s, a gymnast's career was over by sixteen, or whenever her body began to mature into womanhood. My mom has big boobs, and I was always terrified I would end up with breasts like hers, which would also kill my career. I had a belief that if I didn't acknowledge it, then it would not be true. If I trained harder, or lost a little more body fat, my cycle would go away.

When my menstrual cycle began, I told no one. Not my mother, sister, or best friend. I stuffed my underwear with tissue and waited until no one was home to steal supplies from my mom's bathroom closet. Anything I stained I threw away, embarrassed and ashamed. When my cycle did not stop, I cursed my body. I had no understanding that my cycle was a powerful rite of passage, that this was a sacred moment in time that should be honored. I now understand that my menstruation is a symbol of my power, my creative life force energy, my shakti energy. The start of a woman's cycle is a sign of their power to create and give life.

I believe much of Western culture is missing this rite of passage ritual. Young girls and women with lack of true understanding are left shaming their bodies, feeling dirty, and being embarrassed. This shame has pushed women to take pills or use devices to avoid having a cycle altogether. Instead of learning about the power of their blood and its connection to their sacred sexuality and feminine power, society has pushed women to hide the reality of being a woman.

It was not until my late thirties that I began to cultivate a relationship with my moon cycle as part of healing my own sacred feminine. I began with language, paying attention to how I talked about my cycle and about myself during this time of heightened sensitivity. It deepened to how I tended to myself during these days. Instead of pushing through and pretending my period was not there, I took a gentler approach. I switched from using tampons and pads to using a period cup and started forming a relationship with my moon blood. In time I fell in love with the deep, bold richness of the blood's color and its aliveness and saw it as the power of life flowing through me. This practice changed everything for me. I no longer saw my blood or my body as a curse or something dirty or disgusting, but rather as pure shakti, pure life force, pure intelligence, and pure beauty. I saw for the first time the sacredness of my cycle and understood the power that blood holds. I am no longer ashamed, and today, I now celebrate this power. This paradigm shift/change in perspective was a big step toward reawakening my femininity and establishing a connection to my sexual and creative nature.

In the writing contemplation section, you will have the opportunity to explore your rites of passage and your feelings around them, and you may even create your own.

ENERGY IN MOTION

One of the goals of the Second Chakra is to expand your bandwidth to feel, process, and "move" all emotions, while developing a more sophisticated, refined palate that indulges in all the flavors of the life force. All emotions are pure shakti, pure energy. They are neither positive nor negative, but instead represent different qualities of the life force. Emotion comes from the Latin root *mot,* which means "to move," or "to move out." Emotions want to be felt and experienced. They want to move, to dance, to flow like water. The problem is, most of us resist this flow. Instead of surfing with the life force, we suppress, deny, and bury our emotions deep in the subconscious and in the tissues of the body. And for good reason! We live in a society that does not honor this energy in motion. Rather, being emotionless is considered a sign of maturity and strength. This creates indifference, alienation, and detachment, when a healthy expression of our emotions provides us embodiment, connection, and power.

Our society's refusal to ride the waves and savor the flow carries the risk of leaving us emotionally unintelligent and disassociated from ourselves and from the pleasures of life. We learn to live in the gray zone, devoid of real feeling, passion, or color. In other words, the erosion of our ability to recognize what we want renders us comfortably numb—the sense that nothing is ever really good or really bad, just shades of *meh*. If someone asks, "How are you?" the answer is usually "Fine." If asked what we want, the answer is usually "I don't know," "Whatever," or "I don't care."

At some point, unconsciously or consciously, you may have shut down the way you felt. Maybe it was because it wasn't safe, or you feared you would not be accepted, or you were told little girls are supposed to be nice or real women don't get angry, and the only explanation for your behavior must be that it's "that time of the month." Instead of honoring our sensitivity, vulnerability, and emotional range as a superpower, many of us have rejected it as weakness. Or maybe your natural feeling states were denied when you were told "there is nothing to cry about," or "it's not okay to feel that way about your sister," or "get over it already!" When this happens, we start to distrust our own feeling states, and instead of flowing, we freeze. When we stop the flow of movement and the emotional charge, the energy does not magically disappear. It has to go somewhere, so it manifests as *body armor*, or habitual tension held in the body, within the neck, jaw, chest, hips, abdomen, etc.

It takes great courage to feel, to fully participate in the continuous flow of life.

To feel is to be with the intensity of being alive. The joy and the terror, the pain and the pleasure, the sorrow and the ecstasy of this human experience. To do this we must be willing to break the dams we have built and let our emotions flow. Just like a painter needs access to all the colors of the rainbow to create her masterpiece, our glorious selves thrive on the oxygen of euphoria and despair, grief, and love.

In yoga, we have a beautiful word, *rasa*. Rasa is the essence, the juice, the tastes of life. All emotions are birthed out of nine rasas; out of these nine tastes, nine flavors. Our palette is made of love, joy, sadness, anger, disgust, awe, fear, bravery, and peace. Like emotions, rasas are not inherently good or bad. Each one carries its own unique spice and its own brilliant message to deliver. We cannot just pick and choose from the emotional buffet. Instead, we can learn to honor the gifts that each emotion, each rasa, brings.

A common mistake we all make is trying to turn our sadness into happiness. What if instead of trying to transform our sadness, we could be *happy* that we can *FEEL sadness*? What if this could be a sign of success, that we are moving toward a fuller embodiment of our humanity as we allow ourselves to feel rather than flee? Knowing that all emotions are energies that tell her about her body and her spirit and her mind, the wild woman gives herself permission to dive into the sadness and learn what it has

to teach her about herself. By going into the *feeling,* not the *story,* she can be transformed.

All emotions are necessary, even the uncomfortable ones. Without our full range of emotional intelligence, we lose touch with what brings us joy and pleasure; we can't decipher how we actually feel or what we are passionate about; we have poor boundaries and struggle to connect deeply to others intimately and find real love.[3]

EMBRACING DESIRE AND ABUNDANCE—MEET GODDESS LAKSHMI

When you hear the word *desire,* what does it conjure in your mind and body? Do you immediately get a twinkle in your eye or a tingle in your body as your imagination runs wild into the realms of pleasure and passion? Do you go to a place of feeling guilt or shame for having desire? Do you believe that desire is something you should rise above? In other words, do you see desire as icky and evil, healing and meaningful, or something in between?

There is a lot of confusion in the world and especially the spiritual world around desire. It is often viewed through a negative lens, and as a lower vibration. Some tell us that "if you were spiritually evolved enough, you would no longer have desires." I recently heard a spiritual teacher speak on the subject and he suggested (jokingly)

that if we were really serious about our yogic path, we should locate the part of the brain that governs desire and *KILL it off*! To me that seems a little aggressive, and the opposite of yoga. If yoga is about true integration and wholeness, why would we want to kill off any part of ourselves? Instead of waging war on the psyche and further denying, suppressing, or killing anything off, let's form an entirely new relationship with desire, one that uplifts, activates, and inspires clarity of purpose and direction. One that acts as a fuel to ignite the fire (the Third Chakra) and becomes a guiding principle for our life and our enlightenment. When you connect with what you *feel,* what you want, need, and what your heart longs for, you become more alive, life has more color and meaning, and you can begin to taste the sweetness of it. Your desires then work to soothe, feed, and nourish you on the deepest level (mind, body, heart, spirit) and—as we will see in the next section— become doorways into the divine. This new paradigm of desire is a form of radical self-care, instead of an obstacle for our growth.

To support this new embrace, let's invoke the energy of the divine goddess known as Lakshmi. Lakshmi is a goddess of the sensual. She reawakens us to our feminine nature. She is pleasure personified. She is boundless joy. She is abundance in all forms, and she embodies all the different qualities of desire. Lakshmi was churned into being (by the gods) out of the milky waters of the ocean over a thousand years. The milk out of which she was born is said to be the sweetness, sustenance, and power that sustains all life on earth.

Lakshmi, like all the goddesses, has many different forms. Today, let's imagine her with eight arms. In several of her hands she holds lotus flowers, which represent the path to worldly fulfillment and spiritual liberation. In other hands she is performing mudras of offering and abundance, blessings of protection and fearlessness that shower our path with every step. She also holds a sacred vessel or a pot that's filled with her divine nectar, known as *soma*. *Soma* is the nectar of the gods, the elixir of life. We can imagine Lakshmi's *soma* as liquid gold, thick and sweet like honey. She is just waiting to pour it into you, down through your crown, bathing your whole body with it. So I ask you, what do you want to be filled with, infused with, and nourished by? As you identify this desire, you unlock the power and therefore the nourishment of Lakshmi.

As we dive a little deeper into the sacred waters in which Lakshmi was churned, we will uncover different types of desire. These find a symbolic home in Lakshmi's eight arms, which each represents a different aspect of the divine and different aspects of desire. Some say all desires arise out of

these eight qualities, and when we learn to savor any of these qualities, we are merging with the divine, merging with the qualities of Lakshmi. These eight qualities or eight desires are knowledge, sovereignty, energy, strength, vigor, splendor, luxury, *and* freedom.[4]

Let's take a look at each one:

KNOWLEDGE: The longing and craving to know, to learn, to understand, to see, to know our own true path, or *dharma*.

SOVEREIGNTY: The power to be the ruler of your domain, the authority of both your inner and outer landscape, to be the queen of your own queendom.

ENERGY: The thirst for energy in all forms. Physical energy, sexual energy, emotional energy, and intellectual energy.

STRENGTH: Wanting to feel strong inside of yourself, both body and mind. To have the mental, physical, and emotional strength to ride and navigate the waves of life. To not only live, but to grow and transform.

VIGOR: The craving for joy, pleasure, enthusiasm, and rapture, to embrace the intensity of life and the ecstasy of living in this body. When was the last time you felt this intensity or allowed yourself to feel the vigor of existence?

SPLENDOR: The longing to shine your light to its fullness, to feel magnificent, and to be a part of the magnificence and magic of life around us.

LUXURY: The desire for comforts of life such as the luxury of time, space, money; to revel in the fabulousness of life; to delight in a healthy body and a healthy mind.

FREEDOM: The yearning to be free from the demons of your own mind, your limited thinking, your own smallness. Freedom to expand, to connect to the infinite, to pure potentiality that knows no limits, knows no boundaries.

When we embrace desire in this way, it becomes fuel for our empowerment. Each of these qualities is a way to truly be nourished by the sweetness and power of life. Picture Lakshmi now, standing before you, offering you her vessel of divine nectar. Allow it to be poured over you, filling every chakra and nourishing every tissue, cell, and organ of your body. Feel yourself being filled by knowledge, sovereignty, energy, strength, vigor, splendor, luxury, and freedom. Keep bathing yourself in the divine nectar, the divine desire; watch how it becomes your self-care! Take a deep breath in and a deep breath out. Join me in reciting her seed mantra, or prayer, *shrim* (pronounced "shreeeeem"), 3 times.

SEXUAL HEALING

Let's talk about sex. Like the many types of desire, sexuality is a taboo topic in society that usually stays between the sheets and carries a negative weight outside of them. But I encourage you to close your eyes, breathe deeply, and become aware of the feeling of your body. There is an electricity that courses through your skin, a hum that sings in your tissues, a buzz of aliveness that accompanies you into this world. You are a deeply sensitive and sensual creature, with hidden places in the body whose sole function is for your pleasure. Your nervous system is hardwired for pleasure, and pleasure is medicine! It aids in the clearing of old cellular memories of pain that are stored in the body. It takes you out of judgment and into ecstasy. The gateway into ecstasy is through the body and the sensual. The senses are portals into pleasure. As you arouse your senses, you get activated and turned on; you wake up and even commune with god. A healthy connection to the sensual leads us to reconnect with the sacred sexual. This INjoyment leads to deep intimacy with self, and from that oneness with self, sacred sexuality is born. This begins with you, with the connection between your body, heart, senses, and spirit that we have already been exploring. From the tantric perspective, sex is not just about doing it! Sexual energy is seen as a powerful creative force inside you that manifests and creates life. Sacred sexuality is about you changing your relationship to sex and beginning to look at it as one of the most sacred things you could do, rather than as a way to get what you want or to fill an empty void.

This was a concept that, as a survivor of sexual abuse, I did not understand. For decades I never understood what the hoopla was with sex, as I did not *really* enjoy it. Don't get me wrong—I enjoyed the kissing, the physical contact, and the bonding, but I *never* experienced the deep, mind-blowing pleasure I saw in the movies and heard about from friends. I am a very sensual person and can easily get turned on through movement practices like yoga and dance, but when it came to sex, my paradigm was totally different. I learned at a very young age that sex was how *I felt loved*. I used sex not as a way of engaging with the sacred but as a form of currency to *feel* something. To *feel* connected, *feel* enough, and to *feel* what I perceived as love.

For a fleeting moment I would feel those things, until the moment came—and it always came—when I would unconsciously shut down. I would disconnect, "leave my body," disassociate from the experience. This was another side effect of abuse. Numb, and unable to orgasm, I would literally just be waiting for the other person to finish. As I became more sensitive, tears would often stream down my face, not from sadness per se, but from the extreme discomfort I felt as I disconnected more and more from myself. I would continually try to "fix" the *feeling* of disconnection with more sex. You have to understand that for me sex meant that I was loved, even if I did not love the other person, and even if they were not nice to me. I had no conscious awareness around sex, my patterns of detachment, or how

my trauma shut down my Second Chakra along with my sexual power and pleasure.

Years of yoga, dance, and meditation led me back into my body and eventually to therapy. I now understand that "leaving my body" was a survival skill my body intelligently employed as a young girl, to keep me alive in the face of trauma. But now this highly refined skill had my Second Chakra and all its beautiful gifts on lockdown to keep me safe (First Chakra). It was keeping me from being able to access, taste, and experience the ecstatic pleasure and intelligence of this woman's body. Everything I am sharing in this chapter and the practices to come (along with LOTS of therapy) are what I have done to heal, to feel, and awaken my feminine power so that I can taste the sweetness of Svadhisthana. To this day, it is a daily practice of tenderness, of self-love, of reclaiming, and softening into feeling my body and all that flows through it. Now, to me, sacred sexuality is about respect, that I know I can say no and I can sing YES!; that I can ask for what I need and not be ashamed of my own body or what it desires. It is about appropriate boundaries, consent, union, letting go, and the ecstatic thrill of connection between my partner and the divine. Sex, along with yoga and dance, are a way I pray in my body, a time I worship the life force moving in me and another.

THE PRACTICES: 7 DAYS OF FLOW

Day One: Altar

Your Water Altar will become a physical representation of "your own sweet place" that you will return to daily for your Second Chakra rituals. Remember as you create your altar that all the ideas below are just suggestions based on things I use in my personal practice. Your altar should be unique to you and ultimately connect you back to the flow, taste, and joy of life and your divine feminine power. Remember before you delve in: INjoy yourself!

Water Altar Essentials

- Something orange (cloth, candle, stone)
- The element of water (holy water, flower essence, water from your favorite ocean, lake, river)
- An item that represents your feminine power

Water Altar Inspirations

- Sea shells, river stones, or even sand from your favorite beach
- Something that represents your womb: pot of creativity, moon blood, jade egg, or anything else that connects you with your sacred sexuality
- Image of Lakshmi
- Written list of your desires
- Your letter to your yoni (see Writing Contemplation, page 77)
- Crystals: carnelian, orange calcite, sunstone
- Oils: jasmine, wild orange, neroli
- Tarot Cards: Temperance, The Moon, Five of Water, Six of Water, Ace of Fire

Refer to the Quick Charts in the Appendix for extended meanings of crystals, oils, and tarot cards.

Writing Contemplation

1. What is your relationship to the sacred element of water? How do you experience the element of water in both your inner and outer worlds?

2. Just like the moon, you have many different faces. Can you name the various faces of you? How do these faces relate to your emotions?

3. The first rite of passage for most women is understanding your moon cycle. The way I shared mine, write about the story of your first blood. Can you recall the physical and emotional details of this time? What is your relationship with your cycle now? If you have never had a menstrual cycle, think on how you marked your initiation into womanhood. If you cannot identify one, can you construct a ritual to now officially honor this time?

Day Two: Mudra—Yoni

The mudra we are practicing today is called Yoni mudra, also known as the seal of the goddess. This mudra brings you back into feeling contact with your yoni, your womb, your creative cauldron, and to your essence of Svadhisthana.

Here are the step-by-step instructions:

1. Find a comfortable seat in front of your altar or lie on your back in *supta bodakonasana* (soles of the feet together, knees wide apart). You have the option to place two blocks or two blankets right underneath the knees for extra support. It is super important that you are comfortable so you can deeply relax.

2. Bring your thumb tips and your index fingers together to create the shape of a downward-pointing triangle. The downward-pointing triangle represents the energy of shakti, the creative sexual energy that invites you into your life-giving power.

3. Let the hands rest on the low belly, your womb, your yoni. The thumbs touching right below the navel, the fingertips touching right above the pubic bone, pointing downward.

4. Close your eyes, if you feel comfortable doing so, and soften your belly. Releasing any holding, restriction, or rigidity here, as you allow your belly to breathe.

5. Take at least 10 slow, deep, *nourishing breaths*, as you begin resting more deeply into yourself.

6. See yourself taking the seat of the goddess here on the six-petaled lotus of your Water Chakra. You are Lakshmi herself, divinely beautiful, abundant, and whole. This is your abode. Inhabit it more fully with each and every breath.

7. Once you feel complete, open your eyes and release the mudra. Take a moment to pause and notice how you feel.

There is a great softness and strength in this mudra as you nurture your womb but also reclaim it as your own. It brings you back in physical, energetic, and emotional touch with the abode of the goddess that resides here in you.

You can also listen to the how-to audio at www.chakrarituals.com.

Writing Contemplation

1. Pause for a moment and breathe deeply with each of the divine feminine qualities: Free. Independent. Wild. Willful. Sovereign, not owned by another. How do these words make you *feel*?

2. How do you relate to the concept of the "comfortably numb"? Do you give yourself permission to feel all that you feel? How has this helped or hindered your life?

3. When we work with the energy of desire as a nourishing, activating, guiding principle, we align with the forces of attraction, devotion, and bliss. Each is a doorway into the divine. As you think about the eight desires of Lakshmi (knowledge, sovereignty, energy, strength, vigor, splendor, luxury, and freedom), how do you relate to each one? Give yourself some time to explore and unite with the *feeling* of each doorway and see which one is calling to you most right now. Name it. What is this desire calling you forth to do?

Day Three: Breath—Shakti Healing Breath

Today's pranayama practice is called Shakti Healing Breath. It will calm and soothe the nervous system while restoring prana, the sacred life force energy and vitality, to your womb. This practice is exceptionally healing for any woman who has experienced any kind of trauma within her Second Chakra. Examples of this kind of trauma could be a result of a miscarriage, abortion, a difficult birth, issues with reproductive health, physical or sexual abuse, or another kind of injury or trauma to this area. Shakti Healing Breath is a regenerative practice that will reconnect you to your womb and work to restore sensation and bring feeling back into "your own sweet place."

You will call upon your powers of imagination and the sweet nectar of the goddess, in the form of radiant moonlight known as *soma*. With every inhale you will drink in this healing elixir, visualizing it as liquid moonlight pouring down through the crown of your head and into your Second Chakra, bathing every cell, organ, and tissue. With each exhale, the warmth of your breath will circulate through the whole of your womb space, melting any places of numbness, soothing any trauma or discomfort that lives here.

Here are the step-by-step instructions:

1. Return to the supta bodakonasana shape (soles of the feet together, knees wide apart) you explored on day two with yoni mudra. Remember you can always place two blocks or two blankets underneath the knees for extra support.

2. Place your hands on your womb in yoni mudra.

3. Invite yourself to soften here. Take one deep *nourishing breath*. Let go of any tension you might be holding.

4. Inhale through the nose, breathing in the healing soma of moonlight.

5. Drink the breath all the way down, to the front, back, sides of your sacral center (this includes your pelvis, reproductive organs, bladder, and pelvic floor).

6. On a slow, deep exhalation, imagine the warmth of the breath circulating through the whole of your pelvis and igniting the glowing embers of a fire.

7. As you feel this warmth, picture the glow of beautiful amber orange inside your sacral center, the color of the Second Chakra being aroused, awakened, and healed.

8. Repeat 6 more times in the flow of your own breath.

9. For the final 3 rounds on the exhalation, bring in the bija mantra for the great shakti power of Lakshmi, *shrim* (pronouced "shreeeem"). Without

straining, and with a hint of a smile, chant or sing the mantra *shrim* for the entire length of the exhale. The sound will help to circulate and vibrate the warmth of the breath through your Svadhistana Chakra, connecting the sweetness and healing power of your voice to the sweetness of your yoni.

Benefits

- Heals disconnection to the womb space
- Brings sensation and aliveness back to your Second Chakra
- Reconnects you with pleasure and balances sexual energy
- Restores the nervous system
- Connects you back to the sweetness of your voice and your womb

You can also listen to the how-to audio at www.chakrarituals.com.

Note

Keep breathing smoothly, deeply, and fully, never straining on the inhale or exhale. Let your belly be soft and fill with the breath. INjoy yourself![5]

Writing Contemplation

1. Every woman has something to heal in her womb. We are all wounded and have experienced some trauma in our

lives. Again, this trauma could include painful/heavy menstrual cycles, sexual abuse, surgery, fibroids, endometriosis, pregnancy, miscarriage, or childbirth. Write a letter to your womb space. Begin with *Dear Womb* or *Dear Yoni* or any name you may have for this area of your body. Bravely give voice to all that is stored in the deep dark waters. Explore the emotions, memories, and your secrets, along with your desires and longings. Be utterly tender and loving as you open into this vulnerable healing space. Finish the letter by telling her how you intend to love, honor, and cherish her now. Once you're done you may want to place this letter on your altar.

2. Pleasure is your birthright, but many of us consciously or unconsciously deny ourselves healthy pleasure. When and why do you deny yourself pleasure? And how can you INjoy yourself more?

3. Love, joy, sadness, anger, disgust, awe, fear, bravery, and peace are the nine rasas, or tastes of life. Which flavors do you tend to indulge in, and which flavors do you tend to avoid savoring?

Day Four: Svadhisthana Body Prayer

Welcome to day four and to your Svadhisthana Body Prayer. This vinyasa sequence is sensual, feminine, and flowing. Feel the movements of the ocean, the waves as they roll in and out, the tides as they ebb and flow inside of you. Arouse your creative energy and feeling body through this pulsating, hip-opening flow.

I suggest moving through this flowing sequence 1 to 3 times on both sides.
You may also follow along with the guided practice video at www.chakrarituals.com.

Start standing at the top of the mat, feet hip-width apart, knees soft, hands to low belly in yoni mudra.

1. Inhale; rock your tailbone back. Exhale; wrap your tailbone under. Repeat 3 times

2. Inhale; reach your arms up overhead. Exhale; fold forward (bend your knees if you need to). Inhale; elongate through your spine

3. Step your left foot back into low lunge. Place both hands to the inside of your front foot

4. Inhale; round your spine, coil up through the belly. Exhale; expand and radiate back into low lunge. Repeat poses 3 and 4 three times

5. Lower back knee, turn right toes out 45 degrees, sweep right arm up and side bend left. Circle your arm down and around 3 times

6. Come into table pose. Begin to circle your hips in one direction

7. Circle hips in the opposite direction

8. Lower down to your belly, take your hands wider than your mat, and come up on your fingertips

9. Inhale, heavy on your pelvis, strong through your legs and wave up into fingertip cobra

10. Exhale, slowly wave back down. Repeat steps 9–10 three more times

11. Wave back into downward-facing dog (remember the transition to the top of the mat from the First Chakra)

12. Exhale; hands to prayer at your heart

Repeat the entire sequence, stepping back with your right leg.

Writing Contemplation

1. Now that you have dropped into your body and the sensual energy of Svadhisthana with your body prayer, let's examine another rite of passage—your first sexual experience. Take some time to write about your first time. Remember, your words are just between you and the page, so be as honest as you can in your reflection. Is there anything here that needs to be healed, forgiven, honored, or rejoiced in?

2. What were the beliefs you were taught about sex from your family, peers, school, and/or religion? Do these beliefs empower or disempower your sexuality?

3. What does sacred sexuality mean to you? Are you comfortable with your sexuality? What does owning your sexual power look and feel like?

Day Five: Meditation—INjoy Yourself

True intimacy and sensual pleasure begin with YOU! When you soften into your own skin, you naturally begin to connect to your juicy feminine essence and energy. This softening meditation is an invitation to INjoy yourself IN your body, IN your own sweet place, IN your life-giving womb. Sensation leads to pleasure, and pleasure is INjoyment. Through the power of touch, breath, and self-love, let's play with awakening pleasure.

You can do this meditation either seated, standing, or lying down.

1. Find a quiet space where you won't be interrupted. Consider dimming the lights, draping yourself in some soft, loose-fitting clothing. Make sure you are nice and warm. It's time to get comfortable, I mean REALLY comfortable, then soften the eyes or close them completely.

2. Place your hands lovingly onto your low belly in yoni mudra.

3. Take 3 deep breaths down into your yoni, into your feeling center. Exhale out through the mouth any stress or rigidity you are holding in your body or mind.

4. Take one hand and begin to lightly brush your fingertips across your forehead ever so slowly, ever so tenderly. Try it several times.

5. Follow the stroke now down along the side of your face, even down the front or side of your neck.

6. Unhinge your jaw, breathe deeply, and even play with letting out a little sound. A gentle sigh, or use the vowel sound *OO*.

7. Notice any tingles of sensation bubbling up, feelings of warmth or coolness as you

continue to caress your forehead, face, and neck with a feather-like touch.

8. Allow your fingertips to further explore and run down your shoulders, arms, and hands. Take your time. Let your hands be soft, like butter.

9. Allow the tension, stress, and numbness to melt as your fingertips gently, lovingly brush, stroke, caress the surface area of your skin. Allow it to feel good. Allow the stroke to nourish you. Give yourself permission to feel good, to feel pleasure, to even get aroused. This is your exploration.

10. Keep breathing deeply down into your yoni; exhale out with a sigh as you extend this feather-like touch to anywhere in your body you would like, from your head, to your heart, to your legs and feet.

11. As you lightly touch, remember: your whole body is sacred. Your whole body is meant to be INjoyed. INjoy yourself here. In your body, with your own sweet touch.

12. Try whispering to yourself, *this is MY body*. This is my womanly body, and it is meant to be INjoyed by me!

13. When you feel complete, take your hands back to your low belly.

14. Take 3 more slow, deep breaths down into your yoni and be with all that you feel.

Pain turns into pleasure, the whole body is honored; keep melting, keep INjoying. You can continue with the mantra *This is MY Body. My body is meant to be INjoyed by me.*

You can also listen to the how-to audio at www.chakrarituals.com.

Writing Contemplation

1. Take some time to write about your experience in the meditation. Describe what and how you felt. Uncomfortable, comfortable, pleasurable? Use your senses to help guide you.

2. As you reclaim your sovereignty, and know beyond reason that your body belongs to you, who you decide to share your body and sexual energy with becomes increasingly more important. Take some time to reflect on your current or past partners. Are they in alignment with your empowered needs and desires? Try making a list of qualities that you would like to have in your sexual partner. If you currently have a partner, you may consider sharing the list with them. If you are single, use this list to discern who you want to hop into bed with or not.

3. From the place of your fully embodied, juicy Second Chakra—make three sexual wishes. Don't hold back!

In the First Chakra, Muladhara, we explored the first pathway to embodiment via physical touch with self-massage. Paying attention to the sensations we feel with each stroke of the hand and palpation of the muscles there is a waking up to *oh, this is my body. I occupy this space, and I can feel that I am in here.* In the Second Chakra, we explore the pathway of movement. Movement is medicine. It frees us of all that is stuck, stagnant, and rigidly held in the body physically, mentally, and emotionally. On the physical level, movement lubricates the joints, literally gets our juices flowing, reduces stress, frees our energy, and brings feeling back to the body through sensations. Through movement, we learn to pay attention to the *oohs, ahhs,* and *ouches,* the sensations of pleasure and pain. We become aware of what areas of the body are resisting movement and where we habitually store our tension, e.g., our neck, jaw, shoulders, abdomen, etc. On an emotional level, movement unlocks trapped energy and power held in the tissues of the body. Movement helps melt the inner icebergs that keep us from accessing our feelings. Moving gives ALL the emotions a safe place to play, to be explored, to be felt, and to be moved, so we can heal. We cannot heal what we cannot feel!

Today's embodiment practice is about getting curious. Curious about how your body moves, pulses, sensates, and feels. I will guide you through all the major joints in the body, one by one, exploring different ranges of motion, types of movement, and tempos. Your job is to drop your inhibitions, get a little wild, and pay attention to all that you feel. This practice is wonderfully freeing, reduces stress, and unlocks your creative shakti power. Before we begin, know there's nothing you can do wrong—this is exploration—so have fun with it!

1. Find a space where you can move freely and playfully and won't be disturbed.

2. Stand tall, feet hip-width apart or slightly wider, with a soft bend to the knees. Find your grounded, rooted stance you established in the First Chakra.

3. Take 3 deep breaths, breathing up and down through the soles of the feet.

4. Start with your **head**. Inhale; look up, stretching the front of the throat. Exhale; bring your chin towards your chest, lengthening the back of the neck. Repeat 3 more times, following your breath. Pay attention to the physical sensations you feel as you move your head up and down. After the third repetition, keep your chin towards your chest and begin rolling your head from side to side. Right ear towards your right shoulder, left ear towards the left shoulder. Notice how the weight of the head helps to release the neck.

5. Moving from the head to the **shoulders.** Inhale; shrug your shoulders up and

squeeze them up to your ears. Really squeeze! Open your mouth and exhale with the sound *ahhh* as you let your shoulders drop. Repeat five more times, a little more rhythmically. Inhale and gather the tension all the way up to your ears; exhale and let it go!

6. Start circling the shoulders both forward and backward. Explore circling one shoulder at a time or both together. Pay attention to what feels good, what might be sore or tingling. All sensations are a sign of you returning home to your body. From circling, we go to shaking. Start to shake, really shake, your shoulders. Notice how shaking the shoulders connects you to your chest, breasts, and **heart**. Shimmy shake it all! How free, how wild, can you allow yourself to get? Let the love pour out of your heart like a nourishing elixir as you shake for 10 more seconds.

7. Pause, witness, and feel.

8. Let's take it to the **elbows**—yes, your elbows; when was the last time you've paid attention to them? See a theme here? Explore moving them in all directions: forward, backward; make spirals, straighten and bend them. For a few more moments, get fascinated with your elbows and let them lead your dance!

9. From the elbows we travel down to the **wrist, hands, and fingers.** Begin by

MOVEMENT AND MUSIC FOR YOUR EMOTIONS

Play with each of the below movements for 60 seconds:

- Shaking to release fear, anxiety, and heaviness.

- Kicking and punching (the air or a pillow) to release anger.

- Circling, spiraling the hips and pelvis to awaken pleasure and play.

- Heavy sighs and movements of the chest (creating space in the chest) to release sadness.

- Jumping to access joy and happiness.

- Swaying with hands on your heart to access love.

- Experiment not just with your movements, but by using music to support the full dynamic expression of your energy in motion. For example, try drumming for the shaking, soft sensual sounds for the circling, hard vocals or driving beats for the kicking and punching, and wind instruments, strings, or soft vocals for the swaying. Just explore and have fun with it!

circling the wrists in both directions and moving to hula waves with the hands, bringing some wave-like fluid movement into the hands. Lastly, shake your wrists vigorously. All the tensions you hold in your hands, let it all go!

10. Let's take it to the **pelvis,** your entire sacral region, and your womanly **hips!** Circle your hips in one direction. Start slowly, making the circles as big and wide as you can. Then slowly begin to speed it up. Switch directions. Imagine you have a paintbrush right at the end of your tailbone; roll your pelvis forward and back, creating beautiful spirals and waves. Last but not least, start to bring in the shake! Let your hips swing wildly, let your booty bounce, and free up all the energy that is stored here. Allow it to feel good as you awaken your body. Pause, be present, and feel the pulsation of life flowing through you.

11. Bring some of this goodness into your **knees.** Bend your knees, placing your hands on them, and circle them 9 times in each direction. This acts as a healing massage for your knee joints.

12. Let's take it down to the **feet.** Stand on one foot (you can use the wall for support) and roll each ankle in both directions 9 times.

13. To the **legs:** one leg at a time, shake it out, from the very top of your thigh down to your toes; let all your fleshy bits shake!

14. Let's take this shake now into the whole of the body! Your whole body is shaking; you should be sweating now, just 30 more seconds, so let it go! Unleash what is inside you! Give these feelings a place to play. INjoy your home!

15. Take a moment to ground your feet just as we began. Bend the elbows and turn the palms up as a way of "catching" the energy. The transition is the most powerful part. Finish the practice by being attentive to all that you feel in your body. The sensations, the pulsations, the currents of energy, and the life flowing through you. Feel the flow of your emotion, the awakening of desire, and even the hum in all your "secret" places!

You can also listen to the how-to audio at www.chakrarituals.com.

Writing Contemplation

1. What was your biggest takeaway from the embodiment practice? Is there anywhere in your body you were resisting moving? Where do you hold your tension, where are you locked up, and where did your body flow freely?

2. The fourth and final rite of passage is menopause and becoming the wise woman or crone. Crone means wisdom gained through life experiences and also means "crown." How do you imagine your womanhood transitioning if you

haven't experienced menopause? Is it something you welcome or something your fear?

3. Deepen your relationship with the sacred gateway to your divine feminine power, your pleasure, and desire by taking the time to look at your yoni. Yes, with a mirror in hand, can you honor, accept, and love this part of you? Then grab a piece of paper, and take your pen, colored pencils, or paints to the paper and creatively express your abode of the goddess.

Day Seven: Lessons from Your Own Sweet Place

- Your body belongs to YOU.
- Pleasure is your birthright.
- Feel what you feel. Explore your full emotional palette.
- Desire is radical self-care; let it nourish you!
- Honor and celebrate your Rites of Passage.
- Your sexuality is sacred.
- Sex is not just about doing it; it's about worshiping the life force in you and another!

You have reclaimed your most natural craving to INjoy your body, to flow and feel what it feels; you have aroused your senses, said yes to desire and pleasure and tasted your sexual power. Now we are ready to move from Water to Fire, to leave the path of least resistance behind, and to take action. Your passion and desire will act as the fuel to ignite the sacred flames of transformation in the Third Chakra!

Today is your day of reflection and rest. Take some time to reflect upon your most important takeaway from this chakra chapter. If there was only one thing you could remember from this chapter, what would it be? Maybe take a moment to note it down as we continue the journey, that one thing that you want to remember. Now is also the perfect opportunity to return back to any of the previous days' exercises or readings.

"I am immersed in the flame—
The flame of time,
The flame of love,
The flame of life.
The universal fire flows through me."
Step into that fire wholeheartedly,
Starting with the big toe,
Then surrendering everywhere.
Only the not self,
Which doesn't exist anyway,
Burns away.
Attend to this continually,
And awaken into tranquility.
Your essence is renewed in the flame,
For it is flame and knows itself as flame
Since the heartbeat of creation.

—THE RADIANCE SUTRAS: SUTRA 29

5

Ignite Your Inner Fire

THE THIRD CHAKRA

I usually tell my students that you shouldn't have a "favorite" chakra—that each of them is sacred—but if favorites *were* allowed, the Fire Chakra would probably be mine. It's not just because of my fiery hair; that my nickname as a little girl was "red fire"; or that, as an adult, people began calling me the "fire goddess." The element of fire is special—it is the great transformer. It is the only one of the five elements that does not exist in its natural form. Think about it—earth is the ground we walk on, water is flowing in our oceans, air is in our atmosphere, and space surrounds us all the time, *but fire only exists through transformation*. The only way to create fire is through friction—by applying pressure, by building heat, by rubbing two sticks together until a spark ignites.

I'll warn you now . . . nothing about this chakra is passive. You're going to rub up against your own fears, laziness, inertia, and self-doubt—and not just until you smell the smoke. You're going to keep rubbing until you ignite a spark. A spark of change. A spark of action. A spark of recognition so that you can remember *who you really are*.

This chapter will ignite your Inner Fire. The daily practices will fan the flame. Once your Inner Fire is burning bright, you will have the confidence to trust yourself. You will source your power from within. And most importantly, you will build the courage to say YES to the big dreams in your life.

Let's get started.

In its essence, the symbol for the Fire Chakra represents power and manifestation, but not just any kind of power—a deep inner power that arises from our willingness to transform. The shape of the downward-pointing triangle (remember the triangle you created with Yoni mudra) expresses the energies of *shakti* and *manifestation*. Shakti is the sacred feminine—the creative, dynamic power of the universe.

Manifestation is the ability to ground that expansive power into physical form. This makes the Fire Chakra symbol a visual representation of taking our broad visions of unlimited possibility and condensing them with direction and intention until everything is distilled into a single point of clarity and purpose, which is portrayed by

the bottom point of the triangle. If we stay only in the realm of unlimited potential and possibility, we'll never get anything done. But when we get specific and refine our big dreams with focus, intention, and direction, a flame is ignited. That flame is depicted by the symbol in the center of the triangle, or the Hindu symbol for the rising force of freedom, the upward current of liberation. The downward-pointing triangle and the upward-rising flame work together, grounding and condensing the energy from spirit until the pressure gets so strong that it ignites into a flame of transformation.

It is through this cyclical process that we are finally able to live in our authentic power, which is expressed by the small dot above the triangle (the *bindu*). Your authentic power can only arise when you've gone deep within, ignited your Inner Fire, and burned away anything that's not aligned with your truth. This symbol is always depicted in a golden yellow color, evoking the sun and the brilliance that lives within all beings.

YOUR CHAKRA CHEAT SHEET

Name	Manipura	**Bija Sound**	RAM
Meaning	Mani (jewels, riches) Pura (place)	**Vowel Sound**	OH
Physical Location	Solar Plexus (aka your abdomen)	**Energetics**	Power, energy, vitality
Element	Fire	**Affirmations**	Power Lives In Me. I say YES! I reclaim my power now. I Can and I Will. I am worthy! I am enough!
Color	Golden Yellow		
Sense	Sight		

Body parts related	Organs of digestion (metabolism), pancreas (sugar), adrenals (vitality), core (strength and efficiency), liver (anger).
Effects of Deficiency	The light has been lost. Low energy, depression, attraction to stimulants (coffee, cocaine, etc.). Will is weak, breaking commitments to yourself and others, easily manipulated by others because you don't speak up for yourself, difficult time making a decision, and trouble saying no. Cold body temperature and also cold emotionally. Weak, passive, or passive-aggressive. Tendency to make yourself small and to always go behind the scenes. Lack of direction, purpose, ambition. Victim mentality. Not in touch with anger. Often says, "I don't care, whatever you want."
Effect of Excess	Hyperactivity, burning at both ends, uncomfortable being still, unable to relax, attracted to both stimulants and sedatives because of trouble sleeping. Inauthentic expression of confidence. Overly aggressive, controlling, manipulative, arrogant, hot-headed, and power hungry (will do whatever it takes to achieve a goal—lie, cheat, etc.). Stealing ideas from people. Anger issues (aggression, temper tantrums).
Balance	Self-confident, self-motivated, connected to center, aligned with purpose, courageous, able to take risks, playful, spontaneous, and radiant! Resourced with enough energy to meet the challenges of life and say YES to your dreams.

The five energetic principles of the Fire Chakra empower us to see the world differently. When we take off the mask of our fear, shame, jealousy, and self-sabotage and begin to live in a place of will, confidence, and power, we are finally able to live at our full potential. Although there are countless ways the Fire Chakra can impact your life, my experience working with thousands of women from all over the world has shown me that these five energetic principles are the most important. And although I'm separating each principle into its own category, it's important to remember that they are all connected to one another. Read carefully and examine your relationship to each principle. Be honest with yourself—because when we begin the daily practices, you'll have the opportunity to face your long-held beliefs and transform them into empowerment.

1. **Power**

If you could boil all of the teachings about the Fire Chakra down to one word, it would be *Power*. Power is energy. Power is vitality. Power motivates us to take action. From a place of power, we build *will, confidence,* and a *healthy connection to our anger*. But to have the purest sense of power, it must be sourced from within.

A powerful woman knows who she is. She is not afraid to be too big, too wild, too heart-centered, or too emotional. In fact, she knows she can never be "too much." She has her roots firmly connected to the earth, and she is connected to the infinite above. She is courageous—unafraid to go deep within her being to ignite her fire and shine light upon her shadows. It is from here that she can come into full acceptance of *all* she is, denying no part of her exquisite, wild nature. A powerful woman is unapologetic in her efforts and goes after what she wants. She is not afraid to fail, as she knows that each failure tempers her sword and strengthens her vessel. She doesn't have to try to shine her light—it radiates from within effortlessly. So the world sees her fire, and it inspires, supports, and uplifts other women every step of the way. This is how the mere presence of a woman in her power can change the world.

This is the image of a powerful woman. This is what we have the power to become. It's not a dream or a fantasy, but the true potential and possibility that can awaken through the full embodiment of the chakra system.

Unfortunately, most of us have had unhealthy models of power drilled into us from a young age. For example, status, name, and fame—often based on what street you grew up on, what college you went to, what car you drive, and how much wealth you've accumulated—are supposed to indicate your worth as a human being. Or the "top-down," patriarchal model of power, which is all about fear, dominance, and control. It says: *If you don't go to church, you'll go to hell. If you act out in school, you'll go to the principal's office* or, essentially, *Do what I say and you'll be rewarded; if you don't, be ready for trouble.* This top-down model breeds perfectionism, shame, and self-judgment because our worth gets tied to seeking approval from others.

As women, we know innately that this model doesn't work. It causes us to push things down, hide parts of ourselves, and detach from our emotions. To use the language of the previous chakra, this patriarchal model disconnects us from our greatest power—our shakti, or the feminine creative power of the universe. When that connection is lost, we grow comfortably numb and overcome with unworthiness because our worth as women now stems from how well we can fulfill others' expectations of us. What I want for you is to have unwavering power that isn't tied to achievement, approval, or validation. Because if you're sourcing your power from the external, what are you left with when those things are taken away?

The Fire Chakra offers a new model—power sourced from within. Power not just for the sake of power, but to *serve your purpose.* Power that reminds you of the dynamic, creative, and beautiful being that you really are. Power that allows you to rest in your truth, because you know you're supported by the universe.

We all have this power inside of us—so the big question becomes, "Who do you want to become?" The choice is yours. Do you want to be a mom? Do you want to create art? Do you want to be a compassionate and badass boss at work? Do you want to step up your self-care game?

What do you want to do with the power within you?

Don't worry, you don't need to have it all figured out just yet. Together, we are going to use the daily ritual practices to burn our unhealthy models of power in the fire of transformation, so that we can feel the aliveness and the gift that is *ourselves.*

2. Will

As I mentioned in the last section, power for the sake of power is useless. It just feeds our ego. But when we add the secret ingredient of *purpose* to *power,* alchemy occurs, and a new ingredient is born—will. When you're serving a purpose that is greater than yourself, a purpose that *means something* to you, suddenly you gain the strength and courage to move beyond your fears and limiting beliefs and take action.

When I hear women say they "don't have the will" to do something, it usually means their spark hasn't been fully ignited. Will is the catalyst to feed that flame, and it requires a direction and intention to roar into our purpose. In other words, will is the opposite of passivity. It's not about sitting back and waiting to see what someone else tells you to do—will comes from within. Will requires dedication. It requires commitment. It requires courage— courage to stand in the fire, courage to face your fears, and courage to transform. Will asks you to show up every day and do the work.

In the classical yoga tradition, there's a concept called *tapas*. It's derived from the root *tap*, which means "to burn." The practice of tapas evokes a fiery discipline, which I've always equated with *will*. In a vinyasa yoga class, practicing tapas might look like holding Warrior 1 pose for five minutes straight without moving—trust me, you'd definitely feel the burn. In our lives, tapas is the day-to-day practice of showing up with a commitment to your goals—it is through that practice that radical transformation occurs. Your will and dedication are essential. Without them, you'll never create enough friction to burn through your own inertia.

That's exactly why I've structured *Chakra Rituals* in this daily practice format: by completely committing to

do the guided practices, you start to strengthen your will. As you apply your will to this book, you'll build strength in every part of your life and begin to attempt things you never thought were possible—things you never knew you were capable of. By practicing tapas, you will burn away the obstacles that are out of alignment with your life and free up your energy to not only move in the direction of the dreams and goals that have been on your to-do list for years, but finally get them done.

Will also empowers us to stop playing small. It dispels the limitations that keep us from stepping into our dreams— whether it's *I'm not smart enough, I'm not the right age,* or *I don't have the financial means*—all internal and external obstacles become surmountable when we exercise will. We start to believe in ourselves.

The statement *I will* ignites power. *I will* write this book. *I will* start to meditate. *I will* go to the gym. *I will* go after my dreams. *I will* overcome. I *will* heal.

When our *personal will* aligns with *divine will*, magic happens.

Let me give you a personal example. For seven years I managed Exhale Center for Sacred Movement, one of the most well-known yoga studios in the United States. The studio was the original home to some of today's most renowned yoga instructors, including Shiva Rea,

Seane Corn, Erich Schiffmann, Saul David Raye, Annie Carpenter, Sianna Sherman, and more. I was secure, I was comfortable, I was working in a field I loved, and I was in a position of power. People thought I had my dream job. And for a period of time, I did. But things changed. I came to a breaking point, one that many women arrive at: I was no longer happy, I didn't know why I was doing it anymore, and I couldn't figure out how I even got there in the first place. When I checked in with my intuition, the truth was clear—I needed to leave. My soul longed to be teaching and sharing my gifts, not hiding behind a desk and managing other people's careers. But the fear of the unknown was too paralyzing. What if I failed? What if I lost my "power" and status? What if I couldn't make enough money to pay my bills? We've all experienced this type of fear and self-doubt in different ways, whether it looks like the fear of leaving a dead relationship, quitting a comfortable job, moving to a new city, or pursuing a secret dream, because we don't know what life is going to be like after we make that change. But sometimes, building our power requires us to leave the cloaked numbness of safety and comfort and move into a space of *not knowing*. When we throw something into the fire, we never know how it's going to come out on the other side—the transformation is up to the universe. This requires the ultimate trust and being *willing* to take a chance.

It wasn't until my *will to leave* got stronger than my *fear to fail* that I was finally able to take that leap, leave my job, and step into the life that was waiting for me. Today, I'm so grateful to say that I'm no longer behind the scenes. I'm living boldly and wildly in my truth and have the honor of helping thousands of other women do the same. But to gain that courage, I had to step into the fire.

The only way for our will to get stronger is to take action.

It's like a muscle. And as your will strengthens, you begin to recognize your magic, acknowledge yourself, and build even more energy and power. When you take action again and again, you generate *mastery*. You build a deep trust in yourself and in your Inner Fire. This gives birth to every woman's most powerful trait—confidence.

3. Confidence

By now we've all heard the word "confidence" thrown around in every self-help book, spiritual workshop, and social media meme hundreds of times. And although I want you to look in the mirror and know how beautiful, smart, sexy, and fabulous you really are, true confidence is deeper than that. *In the simplest terms, I believe confidence is having unshakeable trust in yourself.* Even if everything else fails, I want you to know you have your *own* back.

As we build trust in ourselves, our capacity for spiritual growth also expands. When we become more grounded, centered, and aligned, we build a clearer connection to our higher self, intuition, and instincts. Think about it . . . that's why we call it a "gut instinct." The most powerful moments of intuition always hit us at the center of our being. But if we've lost power in our center, it's easy to get caught up in insecurities and self-doubt and dismiss our instincts, missing the opportunity for deep spiritual growth. Being connected to your center means being connected to spirit. Both are essential to your liberation.

There are three golden rules to follow when it comes to confidence.

Golden Rule #1: *If you want to build confidence in yourself—you have to stop blowing yourself off.* Every time you break a commitment to yourself, you are strengthening the muscle of *self-doubt.* When you say you're going to wake up early to go to the gym but push the snooze button instead, you're strengthening your muscle of self-doubt. When you say you're finally going to start working on that creative project but keep putting it off to take care of other people, you're strengthening your muscle of self-doubt. We often think of these ordinary moments as harmless, but they're not—anytime you

half-ass your commitment to your goals by not applying your will, you reinforce self-doubt. Most of us women worry so much about keeping our commitments to others but abandon our commitments to ourselves. You will never build true confidence that way. I want you to shift your focus inward. Tend to the relationship with yourself as you would with a best friend or lover. Put yourself first, carve out time for you, and build a bedrock of trust deep in your core so that you can radiate confidence from within.

Golden Rule #2: *Get inspired, don't get jealous.* In the age of social media and the constant portrayal of perfection, it's easy to get lost in the comparison game. Don't! It's a trap. We watch other women's successes, and wonder, *Why did it happen for them and not for me? How did* she *get married, and I'm still single? How do they have the money to take those fabulous trips while I'm here watching them on Instagram?* All of that can be incredibly self-defeating. But if you can change the lens through which you're viewing other people's successes, it won't drag you down. Instead, we can say to ourselves, *by them achieving it, I know it can be done. It is possible!* This builds confidence. Remember, there's no such thing as an overnight success. You don't know how many hours and how much sacrifice someone put in to achieve their goals. They've likely been exercising their will and sharpening their mastery day after day. But all you see is the end result. So next time you watch another woman accomplish something incredible, do not extinguish your inner fire with jealousy— celebrate her success and allow it to ignite your flame of possibility and say to yourself, *I will get there someday!*

Golden Rule #3: *Take compliments more easily than you take criticism.* Although we don't want to source our validation from external sources, sometimes our light gets dim and we forget who we really are. We forget our magic. We forget our gifts. And we begin to doubt ourselves. It happens to all of us. In those moments—when you can't trust the voice inside of your own head—you must stay receptive and open to positive encouragement from *the right people.* It's so easy to let harsh criticism stick to our spirits. But when someone gives a compliment, I watch many women deflect praise instead of letting it sink in. Next time someone gives you words of encouragement, feel it. Allow the words to rekindle your fire. This isn't about boosting your ego—this is about belief. It's about being vulnerable enough to receive. When your faith is shaken, allow other people's love, support, and belief to lift you up and reignite your fire.

All of the concepts we've discussed in this chapter thus far are tied together. Without igniting your power, you'll never generate courage. Without courage, it's impossible to apply your will. And if you don't have a strong will, you'll keep pushing the important stuff off until tomorrow, which takes you further into self-doubt and inaction, dampening your fire and waning your confidence. This is why the Fire Chakra ritual practices are so important. They're about more than just wishing and thinking, they're about taking action so that you experience the deep confidence that comes with *mastery of self.*

4. Healthy Anger

Many spiritual communities say that we should "evolve beyond" our anger, which causes us to suppress our emotions and judge ourselves. Anger is a powerful emotion that should never be ignored. Think of anger as trapped power. When we learn to digest this power in a healthy way, we can use it as fuel to take positive action in our lives. If you remember anything from this section on anger, I want you to remember this:

Anger that's not expressed out, gets expressed in.

If anger is not felt and expressed in a healthy way, it gets stored in the tissues of the body, creates blockages, and becomes a destructive force on the body, mind, and spirit. Sometimes this destruction shows up as self-attack, shame, or blaming ourselves instead of holding other people accountable. This shuts down our energy and erodes the spirit. Instead of trying to push down our anger, we must explore it more deeply. What is underneath it? What does it need? How can we harness the power of its energy? We must become intimately connected with our anger and find a constructive outlet for it to be expressed. This is especially important for women. Anger isn't a bad thing. Healthy anger helps us rise up. It helps us stand up to injustice and take action for the greater good of our world.

If you're deficient in your Third Chakra, it might be hard to get in touch with your anger. So when your fire gets ignited, don't be surprised if you stumble upon some unprocessed anger that needs to be transformed and released. When we ignite our Inner Fire, we can turn anger into action. We can be proactive instead of reactive. And we can channel our healthy anger to serve our growth and take our power back.

5. Self-Sabotage

In 2013, I was on the verge of something huge. For years I had dreamed of creating an event that merged my love for dance and yoga, and the time had finally come to bring this dream to life. I partnered with one of the world's most well-known house music DJs, Marques Wyatt, to create an event called Deep Exhale—a fusion of yoga, dance, and house music that empowers people to experience radical power and soaring freedom. It was unlike anything else that existed in the yoga community at the time. Picture this: it was the overcast morning of our very first Deep Exhale event, which was completely sold out. I was nervous because I had never taught an event like this before, so I decided to go surfing. I thought it would help me get into my body and build some power before the big night. It was a cold day, and I hadn't surfed in a couple of months. As I looked out over the ocean, with my board in hand, I knew the water was a little choppy, but decided to get in anyway. I jumped in, paddled out deep, and within minutes, disaster struck. I caught a bad wave and crashed into the rocks. I hurt myself so badly that a man had to help me out of the water, and I could barely walk to my car. As I sat in the driver's seat in pain and shock, I heard a voice in my head say, *Oh my God, you have to cancel your event.* But at the same time, I heard another voice saying, *But Cristi, this is what you've always wanted.*

In that moment, I had to make a choice. I could let the voice of sabotage take me down its destructive path. Or, I could throw my fear into the fire and allow it to transform into power.

These moments happen to all of us. Oversleeping on the morning of an important meeting, getting sick on the day of a big presentation, or creating some other kind of disaster just before the pinnacle of success.

Sometimes, it doesn't matter how bad you want something; if you try to take action but you're not in alignment, or you don't believe you deserve the success on a deep and unconscious level, you'll do things to sabotage it. But when your Inner Fire is strong, you'll have enough belief and confidence in yourself that you'll beat self-sabotage to the punch. In that seminal moment in my car—bruised and banged up, afraid, and stuck in uncertainty—I made a choice. I decided to step into the fire. For me, it looked like calling my healer, taking some pain medicine (which I never do), and sucking it up so that I could teach the event of my dreams. Years later, Deep Exhale, which I almost cancelled, has propelled me to teach yoga and dance fusion to tens of thousands of women around the world and to live the life I wanted. Just imagine if I had cancelled. . . .

These are the moments of transformation. These are the moments where your practices count. These are the moments when your well of courage, will, power, and trust matter most.

MEET DURGA: THE GODDESS OF THE FIRE CHAKRA

In the world of female superheroes, we have women like Storm; Xena, Warrior Princess; Wonder Woman; and She-Ra as the models of ultimate feminine power. But there is a goddess that supersedes all of these mythical characters. Her name is Durga, and she is the most powerful goddess of the Hindu pantheon—the great mother of all.

The name *Durga* means "she who shines." Her intrinsic nature is fire, which is why I deem her the ruling goddess of the Third Chakra. Durga teaches us the difference between *the power of love* and *the love of power*. That we must always use our fire to help the greater good of the world. Durga is the goddess of strength, bravery, courage, compassion, and anger embodied to overcome injustice—but all in the name of love.

Durga has lustrous dark hair and glistening skin. She rides astride a lion and wears the most beautiful saree, gold jewelry, and always the hint of a smile. At first glance, you would never guess she would be a fierce warrior, but she is the true embodiment of feminine power. In fact, Durga is often depicted with anywhere from eight to eighteen arms. Each of her hands holds a special item from her arsenal of weaponry, specifically designed to alleviate all suffering—to free us from the demons and limiting beliefs that plague our own minds. The best thing about Durga? She *always* comes whenever she is called. We turn to Durga when we don't know where else to go. When we're lost in the web of our fear and self-doubt, we offer it to Durga. With one slice of her sword, she can cut through anything that binds us. Durga is all-powerful: she saves the world when no one else can. Of the many stories about Durga, this is one of my favorites.

Once upon a time, there were two demon brothers named Shumbha and Nishumbha who were granted the gift of invincibility. But to attain this favor from the gods, they had to name at least one thing that could kill them. The demon brothers snickered and told the gods, "The only cause of our defeat could be by the hands of a woman, because no woman could ever conquer us!" The brothers were convinced they were immortal and used their power for evil, pride, and personal gain. They stole the sun, the moon, and every star from the sky, until the forces of good were left powerless and fell to their knees. It was clear that no one could defeat the demon brothers.

As the universe was heading toward its final moments of destruction, a god named Indra appeared who discovered the loophole in the brothers' spell of invincibility. So Indra called a meeting with the most powerful gods and goddesses to devise a plan. They knew there was only one who could defeat the brothers—Durga. So the gods and goddesses pulled their resources together and travelled to Durga's dwelling place. When they arrived, they called to her, pleading for her help. They explained that without her, the world would cease to exist. And because Durga always comes when she is called, she appeared—adorned in gold, riding her lion,

and ready to save the world. The gods and goddesses wanted Durga to be armed with not only her internal power, but also with the greatest powers they each possessed. So each deity gave her a special weapon, which she clasped in her many hands as she blazed off to find the demon brothers.

As she approached their castle, the brothers grew enchanted by her beauty. She was the most gorgeous woman they had ever seen. They fell so deeply in love that they sent their servant down to give Durga a special offer: she would be their wife and a queen. So the servant waltzed down to meet Durga and said, "Beautiful lady, my masters wish to take your hand in marriage. You will be their Queen." Durga replied, "Oh, thank you, sir. But one thing I must request. I made a vow that anyone whose hand I take in marriage must be able to defeat me in battle. If your masters desire my hand in marriage, they must come out and battle me first."

As soon as the brothers heard the news, they laughed and said, "I don't care if you have to drag her by her hair, bring her to us at once. She is ours." The obedient servant returned to Durga and attempted to force her into the castle. But as he approached her, she unsheathed her sword and swiped off his head in one clean swoop. Shumbha and Nishumbha watched from above and furiously ordered their countless armies and demon-warriors to battle Durga.

She defeated army after army and demon

after demon without a hair falling out of place. In fiery rage, the brothers finally awoke to who she was and went down to defeat Durga themselves. The battle lasted days as Shumbha and Nishumbha used one of their most unique powers—the ability to shape-shift. And as the battle stretched on, the brothers continued to morph into different forms, each representing the demons that exist within our own minds. But even this was not enough to defeat Durga. Her ultimate powers of love and connection were able to break through every obstacle, weapon, and demon the brothers cast her way.

Finally, Durga had had enough. With a foot on the chest of each demon brother, she plunged her sword into them both and killed them in an instant. And as the legend goes, in the very moment the sword pierced their skin, Shumbha and Nishumbha gazed into the eyes of the Goddess and were transformed by the power of love, even as they transitioned into death.[1]

Durga's story is the true heroine's journey. She reminds us that when we are connected to our center, we are equipped with all the power we need. Her many arms represent the many responsibilities of the modern woman. And even as our minds try to trick us with shape-shifting fears and limiting beliefs, the power of our love within us can conquer all. When you feel lost, I invite you to look into the eyes of the great Goddess. Allow her to remind you of who you really are. Allow her to remind you of your courage, bravery, and ability to bring the best version of yourself into the world. You are the Goddess. You are the wild woman. And your greatest power is within.

THE PRACTICES: 7 DAYS OF FIRE

Day One: Altar

Your Power Altar is the place you will come every day for your fire rituals. As you build your altar, remember that all of the ideas below are just suggestions based on things I use in my personal practice. Your altar should be unique to you. It should be filled with things that inspire you and motivate you to take action toward what you're trying to accomplish in your life. It should be filled with objects that reflect your power so that when you feel small, or start to lean back into your negative tendencies, the mere sight of your altar will act as a compass to bring you back to center. Ultimately, your Power Altar should remind you of who you really are.

Start with the essentials, and then build from there.

Power Altar Essentials

- Something gold or yellow
- The element of Fire: candle, matches, oil lamp
- An item that represents a symbol of power for you

Power Altar Inspirations

- Mirror: a reflection of your own divinity
- Something to burn: white sage, Palo Santo, piñon, incense
- Image of Durga
- Downward-pointing triangle: symbol of radiant Shakti energy
- Written list of your goals and dreams
- Crystals: red tiger's eye, citrine, and pyrite
- Oils: bergamot, ginger, melaleuca
- Tarot Cards: The Strength, The Hermit, The Tower, The Star, The 3 of Fire

Refer to the Quick Charts in the Appendix for extended meanings of crystals, oils, and tarot cards.

Writing contemplation

1. What does it mean to you to be a powerful woman? What does it look like, feel like? What kinds of things does she do? Describe it in as much detail as possible.

2. As you think about the five concepts explored in this chapter (power, will, confidence, healthy anger, and self-sabotage), in which areas of your life do you feel most powerful? In which areas do you feel the *least* powerful? There may be overlap.

3. Write about a time when you felt empowered and alive. What were you doing? Write about it in so much detail that a director could create a movie scene from your description.

The mudra we are practicing today is an energy-charging mudra, known as Agni mudra. In Sanskrit, *agni* means "fire," and it is the essence of power, light, energy, and transformation. When our inner agni isn't tended to, fed, or nourished, we run the risk of burning out, losing our purpose and direction, and snuffing out the spark of our aliveness. Agni mudra is a mudra we can turn to when we are feeling fatigued, depleted, or unmotivated—it will recharge the batteries, rekindle the spark, and reignite the will.

Here are the step-by-step instructions.

1. Find a comfortable seat in front of your altar. Sit up tall, and ground into your pelvis. Allow your hands to rest on your knees with the palms facing up.

2. Take 3 deep *nourishing breaths*, inhaling through your nose, and exhaling through your mouth.

3. Raise your left palm up to the height of your navel. Rest the pinky-side edge of your hand against your belly.

4. With your right hand curl the four fingers back into a fist and extend your thumb pointing upward. Your thumb represents the flame, the element of fire, and is the outer representation of the flame that burns within. Place the right fist in the palm of your left hand, with the thumb remaining pointed upward.

5. Set your *dristi*, your gaze, softly on the flame of your mudra and take 5 slow, deep, *nourishing breaths*.

6. Then allow the eyes to gently close, taking your inner gaze now to the flame within. Picture, sense, imagine, feel the radiance and the power of your inner flame. Bask in its light, be nourished,

and refueled by it. Imagine the light of the flame spreading through the whole of your body healing, transforming, sustaining every part of you, down to each and every cell. Stay here for at least 5–10 more slow, deep, *nourishing breaths*.

7. As you continue to breathe with this energy-charging mudra, you may choose to consider one of these mantras or thoughts:

   I am the power of the light.
   I am the living flame.
   I am sustained and healed by the light of my inner flame.

8. Once you feel complete, release the mantra and take one more deep breath. Then open your eyes and release your palms down. Take a moment to pause and notice how you feel.

Remember it is the light of your sacred flame that heals and transforms and lifts you out of the lethargy and sabotage. Return to this mudra again and again as a way to tend to your inner flame and keep your agni ablaze.

You can also listen to the how-to audio at www.chakrarituals.com.

Writing Contemplation

1. Who has empowered you when you couldn't see your own light?

2. Did the person you identified in question 1 help to rekindle your belief in yourself? If so, write them a thank-you note.

3. Who have you empowered or uplifted? True feminine power is about mutual support and love.

Day Three: Breath—Kapalabhati

This pranayama practice will increase your energy, stoke your confidence, and bring you clarity of vision. Building your Inner Fire takes energy, so learning to harness the power of your breath is essential.

The breathing practice we're going to do together in this chapter will stoke your fire in a powerful way. It's called the kapalabhati breath. *Kapala* means "skull," and *bhati* means "the shining one." If you've ever seen photos of saints or angels, they're often depicted with a beautiful halo around their heads. Practicing kapalabhati will bring out your energetic halo so that your glow shines bright for the world to see.

This breath activates our Inner Fire and starts to shift our energy upward, just like the light of a flame. It purifies and regenerates our whole system, helps you burn through physical and emotional toxicity, and breaks through the inertia that keeps us stuck. Kapalabhati is activating, enlivening, and heating, so get ready to burn, baby!

Here are the instructions.

1. Find a comfortable seat.

2. Bring your hands to your lower belly in the shape of a downward-facing triangle—fingertips pointing down and thumbs touching.

3. With your mouth closed, start to make short, sharp exhales through your nose in a rhythmic pattern—one exhale per second or faster. As you breathe, focus your awareness on making strong exhales. Allow your inhales to be passive. Your core should feel like it's doing a pumping action—on each exhale, the belly moves inward and snaps back toward your spine. The biggest mistake people make when practicing kapalabhati is using too much force and strain. Stay relaxed.

4. Continue the rapid breathing for 30 to 60 seconds, then take a long, deep inhale, and then exhale slowly.

5. Repeat 3 times.

Notes

- You may get a little dizzy or light-headed; that's okay. That's the skull shining. Stop if you need to. Go at your own pace.

- Keep tissues nearby for sinus clearing.

- If you're unable to exhale through your nose, it's okay to exhale through your mouth.

- Do not do this practice if you're pregnant or if you are on your moon cycle.

- If you have high blood pressure or glaucoma, breathe more softly.

You can also listen to the how-to audio at www.chakrarituals.com.

Writing Contemplation

1. By now you should have a sense of what negative habits, tendencies, and thoughts are keeping you from exercising your will and saying yes to your dreams. If these afflictions were demons, what would you name them? For example, *the demon of self-sabotage, the demon of perfectionism.* Be as creative as you'd like. You can even name your demons after someone in your life.

2. Can you identify the most ferocious demon you are working with? What is it trying to keep you from?

3. Can you ask your demon what it needs from you to set you free? In most cases, our demons show their ugly heads to help us heal something.

Welcome to day four and to your Manipura Body Prayer. This empowering sequence was designed to activate your will, stoke your confidence, and get you moving. Get ready to feel the power of transformation as you ignite your inner fire.

Suggested use: Repeat the sequence 1 to 3 times leading on each side. Follow the pictures to come or watch the how-to video at www.chakrarituals.com.

Start standing, feet hip-width apart and parallel.

1. Inhale; bend knees, chair pose. Exhale; airplane arms and lift heels. Inhale; lower heels and return to chair pose. Repeat 5 times

2. Exhale; hinge from your hips to fold forward (bend your knees if you need to)

3. Step your left foot back. Inhale; rise up to high lunge

4. Exhale; make 2 fists, pull your arms down and back as you simultaneously bend your back leg. Inhale; return to high lunge. Repeat poses 3–4 five times

5. Exhale; shift your weight onto your front foot and pull your back knee dynamically to your chest

6. Inhale; step back, high lunge. Repeat steps 5–6 five times

7. Hands shoulder-width apart, belly strong, plank pose

8. Row your right arm back to your right hip, keep elbow close to the body. Repeat with the left arm

9. Knees down, hug elbows in as you bend your arms to lower to chaturanga

10. Inhale; rise into upward-facing dog. Stand on your hands, lift your knees and hips off the ground

11. Exhale; push back into downward-facing dog

12. Step to the top of the mat, roll up, exhale; hands to prayer at your heart

Repeat on the second side, stepping back with the right leg.

Writing Contemplation

Once you've completed the vinyasa body prayer, explore these questions about power, courage, and fire.

1. What is your relationship to your own core? Do you feel connected to your center physically? How about emotionally?

2. Are you in touch with your anger? When was the last time you expressed anger toward someone? If you have trouble expressing anger, what happens when you keep it in?

3. Fill in the blank: I am strengthening my will for _____
   _____.

The fire meditation will likely be different than any type of meditation you've done before—it's an active meditation. On days three and four, you started cultivating a connection to your Inner Fire with the energy-charging agni mudra and kapalabhati breath. Today, you will feel deeply into that fire to release what no longer serves you. If you want to supercharge today's ritual, you're welcome to do a few rounds of kapalabhati breathing before this meditation, but it is not required.

Here are the instructions for your meditation.

1. Come to a comfortable seated position at your altar. Ground down into the earth through your pelvis and rise up tall through your spine.

2. Take three deep *nourishing breaths*, inhaling through your nose and exhaling through your mouth.

3. Rub the palms of your hands together vigorously (recall your fire kindling practice)—this is how you create the friction needed to ignite the sacred spark of transformation. Keep rubbing your hands until they get hot.

4. Once you feel enough heat, place your warm palms over your solar plexus—the space just above your navel. You can massage your hands around this area to send this heat deep into the core of your body.

5. Close your eyes to the degree of your comfort and begin to imagine breathing energy into your solar plexus—with every breath you are fanning the flame of your Inner Fire which in turn begins to burn a little bit brighter and brighter.

6. For the next 5 minutes, I want you to offer up your worries, fears, and limiting

beliefs to the sacred fire. Be specific, and name each offering. As you send it off to burn, say these words aloud: "I thank you, I release you." And imagine your offering burning in the flame. Give yourself permission to make as many offerings as you need during these five minutes. Burn away all that disempowers you or makes you feel small. Reclaim your radiant light. Free up your power through the fire of transformation. Breathe deeply as you release. Keep going until you feel complete.

Come back to this practice anytime you need it. You can always feel free to add it to any of the other daily rituals. This sacred opportunity is always here to help you burn through what no longer serves, so that you can awaken to the expansive power that lives within.

You can also listen to the how-to audio at www.chakrarituals.com.

Writing Contemplation

1. Name three goals that you have for your life right now. These goals can be related to your personal life, career, health, body, relationship, or any other area of life. No dream is too big or small to include. This is about claiming what you want and putting it on paper. Go wild!

2. What would it feel like if this dream were accomplished? Can you bathe yourself in the fire of the excitement of it actually happening? How would your world change if you reached the goals you wrote about in the first question?

3. It's time to make a commitment to yourself. What are you willing to do today to move in the direction of your dreams?

Day Six: Embodiment—Personal Bonfire

For today's embodiment practice, you are going to call forth your power of imagination and visualization—using dynamic body movements to create your personal bonfire of transformation. The first time I did this powerful ritual I was at the Kripalu Center in Massachusetts. I was on my way to lunch and was literally stopped in my tracks by the sound of ecstatic drumming coming from the main event hall. Before I knew it, I had made my way onto the main floor with 100 other people. I was dancing wildly, and felt so free as the instructor guided us through a metaphorical fire ceremony. The entire experience blew me away, so much so that I not only stayed to meet the creator, Toni Bergins, I rearranged my entire travel schedule to go study with her months later. The body of work she has founded is called JourneyDance™, a transformational embodiment practice to help people move into a new story. Today, we are going to explore a ritual inspired by Toni's genius to help you activate that fire within.

Get ready to play!

Here are the step-by-step instructions.

1. Find a space where you won't be interrupted for this practice. You'll need plenty of space to move, so if there's anything on the floor around you, slide it out of the way so you have room to play.

2. Stand tall in the center of your space. Ground your feet into the earth and place your hands over your Third Chakra—right at the center of your core. Take three slow, deep *nourishing breaths*.

3. Begin walking around your space freely, imagining you are out in nature searching for the perfect spot to build your metaphorical bonfire. Once you pick a spot to build your bonfire, walk in circles around it three times—claiming your space.

4. Pretend to gather all the goods you need for your bonfire. Imagine gathering logs, each one representing a fear, doubt, worry, judgment, or limiting belief that you want to burn in the flames. The power of this practice comes with specificity, so name each log with something you want to release. Give yourself permission to imagine and play like a child.

5. Once you've placed all the logs, begin to rub the palms of your hands together vigorously—this creates the friction needed to ignite the flame. Can you feel the heat starting to build between your hands? Let it build.

6. Once you start to see the spark, it's time to light it up, baby! Reach your arms up to the sky and let out a loud "*Ohhhhhhhhhhhh*" (the vowel sound of the Fire Chakra), and imagine all of the obstructions of your ego burning up in the flames of your sacred bonfire. This fire has the power to free you from anything holding you back in your life; let it burn!

7. Now it's time to shake any obstructions out of your physical body. I want you to shake each part of your body individually, starting with your hands. Shake each hand wildly. Then move the shaking up to your arms, your shoulders, and your chest until the entire upper body begins to shake. Then shake your belly, hips, booty, legs, and feet. Shake as enthusiastically as you can—you are waking up the wildness in every cell of your body. Continue shaking for at least 2 to 3 minutes. You can practice tapas by shaking for a few moments longer than feels comfortable. Shake out your perfectionism. Shake out your rigidity. Shake out the blockages and barriers that hold you back from being the wild, warrior, Fire Goddess that you really are.

8. Once you're all shook up, pause. Ground your feet into the earth and reach your arms overhead. Get still. Feel the buzz of aliveness pulsing through your veins as you are bathed in the light of dancing flames. Stand in it. Feel it. Own it. Honor it.

9. Then repeat this affirmation aloud several times until you feel it in your spirit: "I am the warrior. I am the Goddess. I am me."

10. When you feel ready, come to your hands and knees and imagine using your hands to snuff the fire out—tapping the ground with your palms until you feel the metaphorical fire is extinguished.

11. Complete your ritual by imagining taking some of the sacred ash and painting it onto your body—you can smear it across your third eye, your throat, your heart, or anywhere on your body where you feel like you need to be reminded of the power that lives there.

12. As soon as you finish, take out your journal and begin the writing contemplation practices below.

You can also listen the how-to audio at chakrarituals.com.

Writing Contemplation

1. Write about your experience with the practice. I know this was probably a brand-new experience for you, so write about how you feel right now. Remember, there's no right or wrong. You have permission to claim your true feelings. Write about any shift in your energy, your thinking, or how you felt during the ritual. Did you receive any intuitive messages? If no words come to mind, feel free to draw a picture.

2. What is emerging from the ashes?

3. Now that you've burned through the fire of transformation, what are you saying YES to in your life?

Day Seven: Lessons from Your Fire Chakra

- Your Power is sourced from within.

- Magic happens when your personal will aligns with divine will.

- Build your trust within yourself until it is UNSHAKEABLE!

- Remember the 3 golden rules of confidence; stop blowing yourself off, get inspired vs. jealous, and take in those compliments!

- Anger is trapped power in the body that needs an outlet for healthy expression.

- Transformation is hot, and often uncomfortable; don't stop at the site of smoke!

- Durga asks you to stand in your power and unite with the highest power of all—LOVE!

We've spent the last seven days burning through obstructions, stoking our fire, and freeing up our energy. Now it's time to take this energy upward—allowing the fire in the belly to awaken the fire of the heart. From this place of balanced power, we are able to live fearlessly, take courageous action, and live fully in the power of love.

As we explore full acceptance of our power and embrace all that we are, it becomes easier to be in a balanced relationship with one another. In this way, we're not coming to romantic relationships, friendships, or familial relationships from a place of neediness or a desire to be fulfilled—we don't need another person to make us feel like we're enough. Instead, the strength of our Inner Fire empowers us to experience not only deep self-love, but also radical love with all of our relations. When we're connected to our divine authentic power, we see through the eyes of the divine and experience love in all things.

Today is your day of reflection and rest. Take some time to reflect upon your most important takeaway from this chakra chapter. If there was only one thing you could remember from this chapter, what would it be? Maybe take a moment to note it down as we continue the journey, that one thing that you want to remember. Now is also the perfect opportunity to return to any of the previous days' exercises or readings.

There is a space in the heart where everything meets.
Come here if you want to find me.
Mind, senses, soul, eternity—all are here.
Are you here?
Enter the bowl of vastness that is the heart.
Listen to the song that is always resonating.
Give yourself to it with total abandon.
Quiet ecstasy is here,
And a steady, regal sense
Of resting in a perfect spot.
You who are the embodiment of blessing,
Once you know the way,
The nature of attention will call you to return.
Again and again, answer that call,
And be saturated with knowing,
"I belong here, I am home."

—THE RADIANCE SUTRAS: SUTRA 26

6

You Are Love

THE FOURTH CHAKRA

We have reached the center point, the heart of the whole system, the Anahata Chakra. The place where heaven merges with earth, spirit weaves with matter, and the divine masculine makes love to the divine feminine. A dance of opposite forces coming together to bring about wholeness, true integration, and balance. It is through this great embrace of all of who we are that we awaken to the extraordinary power and gift of LOVE!

Love. We all know its power! It is what makes you feel like you can walk on air, heal your deepest wounds, rest in a space of profound peace, and spread your wings and fly! It also brings you to your knees, makes you howl, separates and divides, and builds invisible walls of protection. One of the great paradoxes of the heart is the more open and sensitive it becomes, the more vulnerable it is to being wounded. But what if there was a place that you could go to not only soothe but heal this holy ache of the heart? What if there was a place you could find that did not require you to shut love down or dress up in armor, but instead a place that freed you to love bigger, bolder, and wilder? *Anahata* means "the unbeaten," "the unstruck," "the unwounded," and "the unbreakable." But the very nature of the heart is that it *beats*, it *breaks*, it *bleeds*, and it gets *wounded* again and again. The word *anahata* is playfully pointing to the fact that you have two hearts, not one! The physical heart which handles all the beating and the spiritual heart that is unbreakable and never dies. The spiritual heart is the innermost cave of your heart space, known in Sanskrit as the *hridaya*. This is your personal reservoir of limitless love that you can return to again and again for true healing. Not as an escape, but to be tenderly held, repaired, and deeply nourished on every level. This place that is just for you will never tire of loving you, as its power and compassion are eternal. Where your two hearts meet is the birthplace of *ananda*, the ceaseless, boundless joy of existence. Let's explore the unbreakable you, fall madly in love, make way for the rise of intimacy, and dance with your beloved.

ANATOMY OF THE HEART CHAKRA

The yantra of the heart is represented by a lotus flower with twelve petals. You can imagine each petal to represent one of the sentiments of the heart—joy, lightness, tenderness, grief, sorrow, hope, loss, elation, love, unity, compassion, and empathy. Inside the lotus there is a radiant six-pointed star formed by two interlocking triangles. The six points suggest all the directions in which our heart and love can move, soar, and shine forth and how, like air, the element of the heart knows no borders or limits. Love touches everything, breath lives everywhere. This symbol in Sanskrit is known as *shatkona* and shows up in many cultures and traditions, from Judaism and Buddhism to Hinduism. In all traditions, the six-pointed star points to the integration of opposites. Here we see it as the symbol of the sacred marriage between the divine lovers Shiva and Shakti, with the upward-pointing triangle symbolizing Shiva, the sacred masculine, and the downward-pointing triangle representing Shakti, the sacred feminine. Regardless of gender or gender identity—there are both feminine and masculine energies in each of us—it is here the eternal beloveds dance their way into a harmonious embrace and find balance.

The color of the lotus is green, which represents life, nature, and the interconnectedness of all living things. Interestingly enough, our eyes can see more shades of green than any other color, thousands of gradients; just like there are thousands of ways in which we can love, each shade representing another variety of love that exists.

BREATH OF LIFE

Your breath is the most precious gift you have. You can live for weeks without food and days without water or sunlight, but you can survive only a matter of minutes without air. Air gives you life, power, and vitality; it feeds you with inspiration and connects you with the divine. The yogis believe that when you are born, the goddess exhales into you, simultaneously you inhale, and you are breathed into life. You can imagine it as a divine kiss, an intimate interchange between you and the goddess. Your entire existence from that moment on is but a dance with *her*, with the sacred life force. The great Shakti is intimately present in the flow of each and every breath you take. When you inhale, *she* is exhaling into you, and when you exhale, it is *she* who is inhaling. In essence it is Shakti who is exchanging life force with you 21,000 times a day, in rhythm with the rise and fall of life. Tend to this relationship daily by giving great reverence to the flow of the breath and its wisdom, as this is the most intimate relationship of your life. Honor the ways it moves you, be in awe of its magic, and fall in love with all its endless qualities from its softness and its wildness to its bestowing and receiving of life and love. Your breath is the intersection between moral and divine, between earth and heaven, and between your body and the larger body of life! This dance will continue until Shakti takes the *Maha* (great) Breath, inhaling your final breath of this life.

YOUR CHAKRA CHEAT SHEET

Name	Anahata
Meaning	Unstruck, Unbeaten, Unbreakable
Physical Location	Center of the chest
Element	Air
Color	Green
Sense	Touch

Bija Sound	YAM (Pronounced yum, like yummy) something so delicious, you are singing your heart a lullaby
Vowel Sound	AH (the first sound babies make)
Energetics	Love, Radical Acceptance, Compassion, Devotion, Intimacy, Forgiveness, Dance of Opposites
Affirmations	I love. I am love: Aham prema. I am worthy of love. I love and accept myself completely. I am in love with the dance of life. I am surrounded by divine love. I dedicate myself to the path of love.

Body parts related	Heart, lungs, chest, breasts, shoulders, arms, hands, middle to upper back; circulatory system, respiratory system, lymphatic system, thymus gland
Effects of Deficiency	Cold, depressed, fear of intimacy, critical of self and others, judgmental, lack of empathy, inability to care for or nourish yourself, martyr complex
Effect of Excess	Co-dependent, needy, clingy, loss of self in relationship, bleeding hearts, lack of boundaries, tendency to get over-extended and taken advantage of
Balance	Radical self-love, self-acceptance, compassionate, intimate with self and other. Good boundaries—know when to say NO, empathic, warmth of heart, lover of life

HEART INTELLIGENCE

The physical heart is powerful, intelligent, mystical, and potentially the hardest-working organ in the body. Mystics for centuries have called it the seat of the soul, as, in the womb, you begin to manifest into the physical form through the pulse of the heart. Yes, it is the heart, not the brain, that forms and begins beating first! In the womb the first sound the fetus hears or feels is the beat of the mother's heart. Through the innate intelligence of the heart, the heartbeat of the baby begins to match the rhythm of the mother's, and a bonding begins to occur, as they beat or dance together as one. A similar synchronization happens in our relationships with our loves. We now know (due to decades of research at HeartMath Institute) there is not only communication from the heart to the brain, but that the heart sends more information to the brain than vice versa. Science now proves what the yogis have known for thousands of years, that there is a special intelligence and wisdom that resides in the heart. The heart also produces the largest electromagnetic field in the body, five thousand times more powerful than that of the brain. This power of the heart field is the Anahata Chakra; it not only envelops you, but radiates out from your center, impacting the space around you and everyone in it in all directions up to fifteen feet away.

On the most simplistic level, the work of the heart is to give and receive. On the physiological level, the heart receives blood from and gives oxygenated blood back to the body. On the pranic level, the body breathes in, receiving breath, life force, and oxygen, and gives breath and life back through the carbon dioxide which is exhaled. On the intellectual level, the heart gives information to the brain and receives information back from the brain. And on the interpersonal level of relationships, we dance between giving and receiving love. Our hearts are always giving life, breath, and love and receiving life, breath, and love!

WHERE JERRY MAGUIRE GOT IT ALL WRONG!

One of the single most Heart Chakra–crushing lines ever spoken in a movie was in the romantic comedy *Jerry Maguire*. Jerry, played by Tom Cruise, in his attempt to not let the woman he just realized was the love of his life get away, made a grand romantic gesture to Renée Zellweger's character by uttering the words, "You complete me." This was the moment he won Renée's character over, and simultaneously women's hearts around the world melted and cheered! "How sweet," "how romantic," "this is what I want!" I am here to tell you, NO, it is not! These three little words "You complete me," no matter how romantic they may seem, cripple the Heart Chakra. They imply—more than imply, state—that I am NOT a whole person unto my own and that I NEED another individual. That I am not enough all on my own, and that

only when I find that perfect person who is also incomplete in their own right will I be happy, fulfilled, and whole. Can you now see how damaging and disempowering these three little words are? And how it leads to belief systems warped by codependency? Our ego, of course, wants the grand gesture from our beloved, and that is okay, but the *only* person you should ever be saying "You complete me" to is yourself. The Heart Chakra is first about union, integration, and wholeness: union with all parts of yourself. The inner marriage of Shiva and Shakti, the divine masculine and feminine energy coming into balance. Another person will never be able to complete you, as you are already perfect, whole, and complete right here and right now. And no other person will be able to fill the void or longing in your own heart, as that can only be filled by you, the love of your own heart.

RADHA

The wild woman I designate as the queen of the Heart Chakra is Radha. Just the sound of her name makes me want to sway, sing, and dance with the life force moving through me as an act of the deepest devotion and celebration for life. Radha lives in the current of *bhakti*, of utter devotion, as she longs and yearns to commune with the divine. Simultaneously, she is wildly passionate, sensual, and erotic and will

risk everything for love. Her name means "one who is the form of worship," as she is worshiped by all beings, especially by her male counterpart and beloved, Krishna. Radha and Krishna live in full majesty; they are one soul manifested into two different forms. They are the personification of both romantic love and spiritual love. They are the space in the heart where the physical and spiritual meet, where the song of Anahata is always playing.

Radha is everything. She is both human and the goddess. A dutiful wife and mother, and simultaneously engaged in an erotic love affair with Krishna. She stands in her power and surrenders to God. She is a lover, a queen, a village woman, a singer, a dancer, a rebel, and an introvert. She both lies down at the feet of her beloved and keeps him under control. She is the integration of all things, not one thing or another.

Once upon a time, long, long ago, it was the middle of the night, and Radha was fast asleep. She was awoken by the intoxicating song of Krishna's flute. She got up, tip-toed out of bed and over the sleeping bodies of her family, and went down to the river to make love to Krishna under the moonlight. The night turned into a party, a never-ending festival filled with play, love, music, singing, and dancing. Soon all the village women, or *gopis*, snuck out of their homes to join in on this joyful awakening, known as the RasaLila. If you recall from the Second Chakra, *rasa* means "tastes" or "flavors" and refers to the full range of emotional experience. From happiness to disgust, laughter to peace, and everything in between, all are sentiments of the heart. *Lila* translates to "the divine play." This RasaLila is the dance of divine love. Radha and Krishna are at the very center, and the gopis surround them in a giant circle. But this dance didn't just happen long ago; it is happening within you right now. Each gopi represents one of the "parts" of you and is one of the rasas. They invite you to welcome and name every part of you, from the queen, to the wild woman, the lover, skeptic, the writer, the daughter, the healer, the artist, the bitch—welcome all of who you are into the dance of the heart. Welcome every movement of love, fear, anger, laughter, joy, disgust—invite them in and celebrate them. The RasaLila gives them all a place to play. Can you feel the RasaLila happening inside of you right now? It is beckoning you to come forth. It is through this full-body welcoming and honoring of the whole of you that the Anahata sings her song and dances into balance.

SELF-LOVE VS. KRYPTONITE

Louise Hay, bestselling author and teacher of metaphysics, taught for decades about the power of love. She wrote that at the root of every problem you will find one thing, a lack of self-love, and that the solution to every problem is found in one learning to love and accept oneself fully. Can self-love really be the answer to everything? Maybe not; but as simplistic as it may sound, learning to fall wildly in love with yourself might be the single most important thing you can do in this life. I tell you this as a person for whom self-love and self-compassion have *not* come easy. It is something I have had to work on daily and sometimes even moment to moment. Here is what I have learned from my years of success, failure, and recommitment.

Self-love is your greatest superpower and your lack of self-love, i.e., self-hatred, is your kryptonite. The Heart Chakra (and self-love) sits at the very center of your being, with three chakras above and three chakras below. Every time you abandon yourself, kryptonite insidiously spreads from your center through the whole of your body, impacting every chakra—it corrodes your deep, stable roots, it erodes your ability to trust and to feel, it snuffs out the fire of transformation, it pushes you out of harmony with your authentic truth, and it fractures your connection to heaven and earth. Just like Superwoman in the face of kryptonite, you do not stand a chance!

So what can you do? It starts with the act of remembering who you really are, which is Divine Love. Yes, YOU are divine love. Say it with me in English or in

WAYS TO CONNECT WITH THE ELEMENT OF AIR

The power of the air is what gives us voice, frees us from the imprisonment of the mind, awakens our connection to the unseen world, and teaches us how to fly. This is the energy of new life, new beginnings, the rising sun, the dawn of a new day.

- Get out in Nature. Go where it is Green.

- Walk, run, dance, yoga! Get your heart pumping and breath flowing!

- Move like air! In circles, spirals, take up space, move without restriction and with total freedom! Play with flapping your wings and taking flight!

- Start to form an intimate relationship with your breath. Begin with giving yourself to a single breath fully and completely. Over time, build up to 10 breaths.

Sanskrit: *I am Divine Love, aham prema.* This is my most beloved mantra. Say it one more time, this time without rolling your eyes. *Aham prema. I am divine love.* You were born this way. You did not have to do anything to become love or be worthy of love, because your essence is LOVE. But at some moment in time you forgot this truth, and you began *learning* new ways of being that are *not so loving*. Maybe this manifested as perfectionism with a relentless inner critic that is difficult or next to impossible to silence. Or maybe you learned to put conditions on your love; to hide, reject, or deny some part of yourself. Perhaps you learned self-harm—an eating disorder, drug or alcohol abuse, sleeping with men or women who treated you horribly. Recognize any of these not-so-loving learned behaviors? This is no time to judge; it is time to become aware. Awareness awakens consciousness, and consciousness makes way for choice. Self-love vs. self-hatred becomes a choice. Will you choose to fill yourself with poison or will you choose to activate your superpowers?

Self-love is not a "woo-woo" concept; it is a behavior, just like self-hatred. It is the act of remembering, accepting, and being with yourself moment to moment. It is a practice of paying attention to how you speak, care, support, and honor yourself, and it is truly the highest form of self-care there is. By choosing you again and again and again tenderly, and by treating yourself with the highest respect you deserve, you will start to remember and reconnect with the essence of who you really are, the aham prema. Love is not something you become, it is who you are. Kryptonite does not stand a chance in the face of divine love.

Today I Choose:

- To recommit to falling in love with myself
- To call back the parts of me that I have cast out, denied, shamed, and hidden and I re-welcome all of me to me
- To wake up to the fact that my greatest strength, my superpower, comes from my ability to lovingly care for myself in endless ways
- To unfurl my heart wings and Fly in LOVE

FROM ME TO WE

The journey from me to we began on day one by honoring your body temple in the First Chakra, then by building an intimate connection with all that you feel and desire in the Second Chakra, igniting the fire in the Third Chakra to help burn away anything in your system that is not of love, so that now, you can truly SEE all of who you are and reclaim all the places within you that you have rejected. When you touch this great love inside that is eternal, you taste and feel the wild devotion for self.

From this integrated whole-hearted place, it is time to reach out and touch another.

We are social beings hardwired for connection. We thrive on physical, mental, emotional, and spiritual connections. Connections are what make us feel alive and help us grow and learn the many lessons of love. But in order to have true connection, we have to allow ourselves to be seen, really seen. Here lies the work of intimacy or as I like to say, "into me I see," or "into me I let you see." Sharing yourself with another person may be one of the scariest and most sacred things you can do. Allowing someone to get close enough to really see inside, beyond the masks, the armor, the *I'm fines*, the fear of *if they only knew* this, or *found out* that, or *soon they'll realize that I'm not perfect, and they'll no longer accept, love, or approve of me.* Beyond all that, there's vulnerability. And to be this vulnerable takes tremendous courage. And when I speak of courage, I mean in the original sense of the word, coming from the Latin root of *cor,* which means "heart." Brené Brown, respected researcher and bestselling author, describes courage in the most touching way. She writes that "having courage is to tell the story of who you are with your whole heart." This is the kind of courage I wanted to have, but did not. I always had lots of friends, boyfriends, lovers, and acquaintances. Each getting some part of me, while other parts stayed neatly tucked away. I learned that

looking good on the outside or in the eyes of others was what mattered most. I did my best to do just that; I kept myself looking good on the outside and kept everyone just far enough away that they could not really see what was going on under the surface.

Several years ago, I was caught in a loop of severe trauma and suffered from debilitating PTSD. I hid my pain and struggle from the world. I feared if anyone really knew what I was going through, I would be vulnerable to lose even more. I have not lived a traditional life by society's standards. I have never been married, and I don't have any children. The great love of my life thus far has come in the form of friendship. Friendship with my best friend, Justin. Ironically at first it was him that I was most terrified to let see my brokenness. Sure, he had seen me through breakups and other disappointments, but it paled in comparison to the brokenness I was hiding most of the time. Our relationship was fun and playful—we danced wildly, talked about boys, and took trips to Burning Man. Justin loved the fun, free-spirited Cristi that was up for anything; he also loved the ambitious Cristi who was not afraid to go after her dreams or travel the world. But what would he think about the vulnerable, messy Cristi that was secretly crumbling to pieces? So, despite our closeness, I kept him, along with everyone else, at arm's length, building up my wall of protection even higher so no one could see in. The problem with this technique is that I was left standing *alone* on the other side of my giant wall. In my isolation, I was more "protected" but further from all I loved and whom I loved, which of course debilitated me more. Eventually the wall became so heavy, I could no longer hold it up. It came crashing down like an avalanche.

One night I made my way to Justin's house. I was wailing so hard I could barely speak or breathe. He witnessed me at what I would have perceived as my ugliest. And instead of rejecting me, he grabbed me and held me for what felt like lifetimes and said, "Thank you." I was astounded, "Thank you?!? Yeah right?" He said it again, "Thank you for giving me the privilege of seeing you, in this state and every state. I somehow love you even more." Through this experience, I finally realized that it is my

vulnerability (as uncomfortable and scary as it may be) that makes me strong, real, and beautiful. That vulnerability shows our depth, range, and willingness to really love ourselves, another, and this life. It is what makes us wholehearted wild women!

To love is to be seen. Opening up to true connection is taking a chance. It is spreading your wings and not knowing if you are going to fall or fly. The next time you are standing on the edge of a mountain, not knowing if you should leap or climb back down, remember there is a place inside you cheering you on, daring you to soar. And when you fall, because sometimes invariably you will, the unbreakable part of your wild heart will be right there to catch you, nourish you, and repair you, every time. Have the courage to live, to expand, to contract, to fly, to fail, and to fall. I promise the crash is less painful than the agony of never taking the leap!

THE PRACTICES: 7 DAYS OF LOVE

Day One: Altar

Your Heart Altar will become a physical manifestation of all that you love and all that you are wildly devoted to. This will be a place for you to return to again and again for your ritual practices AND to be reminded that *You Are Love* and *You Are Loved!* Remember, the ideas below are just a suggestion; follow the current of love that flows through you, let it be your guide. Invite all that you adore and all that is nourishing to your heart into your altar of LOVE.

Heart Altar Essentials

- Something green (cloth, candle, plant, or stone)

- The element of air (fan, feather, wind chimes to hear the air moving around you, burning sage or incense to produce smoke)

- Something living (plants or flowers)

Heart Altar Inspirations

- Roses (as roses hold the highest vibration and frequency)

- Something pink, as pink is the vibration of love and can gently help to loosen the tension in the heart

- Your love letter to yourself (see Writing Contemplation, page 133)

- A book of your favorite poetry, i.e., Rumi, Hafiz, Maya Angelou, Mary Oliver, Rupi Kaur, Amanda Gorman, etc.

- A six-pointed star

- Shiva lingam

- Yoni

- Pictures of people you love

- Image of Radha

- Crystals: rose quartz, morganite, aventurine

- Essential oils: ylang-ylang, geranium, helichrysum

- Tarot Cards: The Hierophant, The Lovers, The World, Seven of Water

Refer to the Quick Charts in the Appendix for extended meanings of crystals, oils, and tarot cards.

Writing Contemplation

1. What is your relationship to the sacred element of Air? What is your relationship with your breath?

2. How do you experience love in your life? Do you feel love for nature, animals, Mother Earth, people?

3. Do you give yourself the love you deserve for just being you? Do you treat yourself with kindness and compassion? Do you feel worthy of love?

Day Two: Mudra—Hridaya

Our hands are an extension of our heart and our love, so you could say all mudras are a practice of the Heart Chakra. The mudra we are practicing today is a simple yet powerful one. It is called hridaya mudra. *Hrid* means "of the heart," and *daya* means "compassion." Hridaya is the innermost cave of our heart space. It is the space in your heart that is just for you, the place that you can return to again and again to be nourished, loved, rejuvenated, and healed—the spiritual heart.

Here are the step-by-step instructions.

1. Find a comfortable seat in front of your altar.

2. Take your left hand and place it flat against the center of your chest (on your Heart Chakra). The left hand is the receptive hand of shakti, the sacred feminine, the creative power of the universe.

3. Place your right hand over the left. The right hand is the force of shiva, representing the sacred masculine, the ground of support.

4. Holding your heart ever so tenderly and lovingly, start to massage the heart space by making little circles with your hands in one direction. Allow the movement to help soften the armor and take down any walls of protection. Let your heart know, through this embrace, that it is safe and that you got you.

5. Close your eyes to the degree of your comfort and tune into what is in your heart. What is wanting to be healed, to be tended to, to be acknowledged?

6. Take at least 10 slow, deep breaths here, breathing into the power of your heart.

Inhale from the root of your pelvis into the root of your heart, into the inner cave of your spiritual heart, and exhale out love in all directions.

7. Now, imagine someone you love—it can be anyone, even yourself. It can be someone who is alive or someone who has passed on. Just imagine them sitting behind you with their arms lovingly wrapped around you and their hands making the seal of hridaya mudra on top of your hands.

8. Picture, sense, imagine, and feel the love and support of this energetic embrace.

9. Begin to pulse your hands a few inches away from your heart as you inhale. Pulse them back as you exhale. Repeat a few more times—imagine you are breathing with this person. Feel your energetic field growing stronger and your Heart Chakra spinning open and expanding in all directions.

10. When you are ready, thank yourself or your loved one for joining you. Bow forward and turn the corners of your mouth slightly up, creating the gesture of smile mudra—as the hridaya is the birthplace of ananda, endless joy!

11. Take a moment to transition back and witness all that you feel and all that touched you.

You can also listen to the how-to audio at www.chakrarituals.com.

Writing Contemplation

1. How was love modeled in your family? How have your parental relationships positively or negatively affected your current relationships?

2. We all have heart armor and walls of protection. What caused you to armor your heart? Can you ask your heart what it needs? Ask aloud, how can I lovingly dissolve this armor?

3. For various reasons, we shut down connection to our own hearts and are subsequently cut off from the messages and living intelligence that reside there. The exercise here is in some ways a continuation of the previous question. Tune into your heart and allow her to speak and write a letter to you! You can begin with something like, *Dear [insert your name here], Even though you have built up walls around me, I will never stop loving you. . . . Love, your Heart*

Another translation of *anahata* is "unstruck," meaning the chord of a musical instrument that has never been *struck*, but is always resonating. This is the place where your physical and spiritual hearts meet and spin an eternal love song that plays on and on, whether you are wounded or unwounded. The Breath of Heart technique will guide you into this space.

Here are your step-by-step instructions.

1. Find a comfortable, grounded seat or, if you prefer, you can do this practice standing.

2. Close the eyes or softly bring them to a half gaze.

3. Take your hands into hridaya mudra, left hand to heart, the right hand on top of the left, making physical contact with your Anahata Chakra.

4. Take one deep breath in through your nose and out through your mouth, emptying your lungs completely.

5. Begin to inhale deeply from the root of your pelvis, to the root of your heart for a count of 6. Pause. Exhale out from the center of your heart for a count of 6.

6. Continue like this for 5 more rounds, inhaling from the root of your pelvis to the root of your heart. Feel your heart expand as your breath fills the front, back, and sides of your chest. Pause for a moment and let the energy of your exhales radiate outward like beams of light in all directions.

7. Stay with the breathing pattern and begin to introduce the bija, or the seed mantra of the heart: *YAM*. It is pronounced "yum." Inhale from the root of the pelvis into the center of your heart, exhale out the sound (internally or externally) of *yummmmmmmmm*. Imagine the sound being the most delicious sound you have ever heard.

8. Continue for 5 more rounds. Inhale from the root of the pelvis to the center of the heart. Exhale out with the sound of *yum* as if you were singing your heart the sweetness lullaby.

9. For the last several rounds, you will add a movement with the arms like wings. Inhale from the base of the pelvis into the center of the heart. Exhale; stretch out your arms like wings, sharing your heart-song with the world. Inhale and fold your wings in to touch your heart. Exhale; expand your wings and soar. At first this may feel in opposition to the natural flow of your breath. We are breathing this way so you can feel your reciprocal connection with all of life.

10. Continue in the flow of your breath (with the sound and the movement of the arms) and feel into the intrinsic connection between your heart and all of life. With every exhale, your eternal heart-song radiates and ripples out to your friends, to your communities, to your families, and to all of nature. Giving life and love. With every inhale, feel all of yourself communing with nature and the divine as you receive breath, life, and love.

You can also listen to the how-to audio at www.chakrarituals.com.

Writing Contemplation

1. Who and what makes your heart sing?

2. What does forgiveness mean to you? Can you forgive yourself for the things you have or have not done? Who can't you forgive and why?

3. Write a second letter, this time from the perspective of you speaking to your heart. *Dear Heart, I am sorry that I have not listened or tended to you in quite some time. I am here now. Thank you for not quitting on me. . . . Pour forth all you want to say. Love, [insert your name here]*

Day Four: Anahata Body Prayer

Welcome to day four! Your Anahata Body Prayer invites the healing power of love into your heart and life. This soulful sequence will work to gently open up the chest, shoulders, and upper back, while strengthening your legs. Find freedom in your movements as you massage the wounds of your heart space and unlock the limitless love that resides in you.

As always, respect your body and do the best you can.

Suggested use: Repeat the sequence 1 to 3 times on each side. Follow the pictures to come or watch the how-to video at www.chakrarituals.com.

Start standing, feet hip-width apart, hands into Hridaya Mudra

1. Inhale; open arms wide and lift chest. Exhale; pulse hands back to your heart. Repeat 3 more times

2. Interlace your fingers behind your back. Bend your knees, hinge from your hips, and fold forward

3. Release your hands to the ground. Step your left leg back and inhale; rise up into high lunge

4. Exhale; circle your arms back and around 3 times

5. Interlace your fingers behind your back. Inhale; lift your chest up and back

6. Exhale; hands down, knees down; table pose

7. Extend your arms forward, melt your chest towards the ground, and breathe deeply; anahatasana

8. Hands in prayer, elbows shoulder-width apart; tuck toes under, push down into forearms, lift hips into dolphin pose

9. Lower down to your belly. Interlace your fingers and press your pubis down strongly. Inhale, lift chest and legs into salabasana. Exhale, slowly lower

10. Inhale; rise up into upward-facing dog. Broaden through your collar bones and draw the head of your arm bones back

11. Exhale; press back to downward-facing dog

13. Step to top of the mat, roll up, hands to prayer at your heart

Repeat on the second side, stepping back with the right leg.

Writing Contemplation

1. The Heart Chakra is at the center of our entire energetic system, and it longs to be in balance between giving and receiving. Examine the primary relationships in your life and notice your tendencies. Do you constantly over-give or over-sacrifice to the detriment of yourself? Do you lack boundaries, have a difficult time saying no, and easily lose your sense of self and your center in your relationships? If so, how can you begin to call upon the power of your Third and Fourth Chakras to strengthen your boundaries within yourself and with others and begin to restore the balance your Heart Chakra craves?

2. If you fall on the other end of the spectrum and tend to only take, what would starting to restore balance and softening your boundaries in this direction look like?

3. You receive life and love 21,000 times a day on the thread of every breath you take in. And you also give life and love back 21,000 times a day with the breath you let out. This harmonious relationship happens with an effortless grace and ease. How can this primary relationship with your breath be a living example of all the relationships in your life? What would it feel like to carry this effortless grace and ease into each and every one?

Day Five: Meditation—Bhavana

Bhavana is the Sanskrit word that means "deep feeling state," "devotion," "steeping," or "infusion." In bhavana meditation, you bathe yourself in the feeling quality that your heart craves to be nourished by, longs to be filled with, and wants to merge with. In bhavana meditation you start with what you love!

Let's begin the practice.

1. Come to a comfortable seated position at your heart altar. Bring your hands to your heart, into hridaya mudra.

2. Take three deep *nourishing breaths*, pulsating with all that is in your heart.

3. Ask your heart, *What would you LOVE to be filled with, nourished by, bathed in right now? What quality of the life force energy do you need, long for, or crave?* Don't overthink it, there are no wrong choices.

Peace, clarity, joy, love, shakti, grace, power, sunshine, dark chocolate? Name one to three qualities; usually the first thing that comes to mind is the exact medicine your heart desires.

4. Internally start to speak or sing your quality or qualities on the rise and the fall of your breath. Inhaling deeply, exhaling, repeating your word or words. Continue for several more rounds,

getting to know your quality's unique vibration. Flirt with it, fall in love with it as you bathe yourself in its resonance.

5. Now start to add the movement of your arms. Inhale, sweep your arms up overhead; exhale, palms turn in and hands cascade down in front of your body. Inhale, arms float back up overhead; exhale, imagine the energy of your word or words pouring down over you. Filling every cell, every nerve, every tissue of your body with this heart-healing elixir. Continue with this beautiful breath and movement bhavana circuit for 5 more rounds.

6. After the 5 rounds, return your hands to your heart, to hridaya mudra, and repeat the words *I AM* in front of your quality.

For example: "I AM love." "I AM Shakti." "I AM sunshine." Repeat 3 times. Dissolve in the exquisite bhavana of your heart.

You can also listen to the how-to audio at www.chakrarituals.com.

Writing Contemplation

1. Take a few moments to reflect upon your bhavana meditation. How did it feel to be bathed in what you love? Can you see how your love has the power to nourish and heal you on every level—mind, body, heart, and soul?

2. Make a list of 10 things you love.

3. How are you being called to rise in love and courageously tell the story of your whole heart?

Day Six: Embodiment—FROM ME TO WE

The embodiment practice for your Heart Chakra is going to help you break through your intimacy blocks with yourself and with another. This practice asks you to be vulnerable. It asks you to see and to be seen, to love and to be loved, and to give and to receive. It will give you access to what is in your heart and allow you to share that with another.

For this practice you will need to recruit a friend. This person can be a sister, a brother, a mother, a father, a child, your beloved, your best friend—it doesn't matter. Anyone with whom you feel safe is the perfect person.

Here are the step-by-step instructions that you and your partner will **both** follow.

1. Come into a grounded, seated posture, sitting face-to-face with your partner. You want to sit close enough that your knees are lightly touching. Take a moment to get present together and honor one another in any way that feels comfortable to you—keep it simple. A long hug, eye contact, or a gentle bow. Then bring your energy back to you.

2. Return to hridaya mudra: the left hand to the chest, the right hand on top of the left. Close your eyes to the degree of your comfort and feel into your beating heart.

3. Begin to gently massage the heart, making little circles in one direction. Imagine the circular movement opening your Heart Chakra and giving you access to the innermost cave of your spiritual heart.

4. Take three *nourishing breaths* into the power of your heart, breathing from the root of the pelvis to the root of the heart and exhaling with a little sound. With each breath, feel your chest expand in all directions, front, back, and sides, even feel your heart wings starting to unfurl.

5. Then pause and ask, what is in your heart right now, and what does it need right now? Listen. Breathe that in and out.

6. As we move from ME to WE, keep your left hand on your heart and reach across and place your right hand on top of your partner's left hand, creating this seal of hridaya jointly.

7. Close your eyes and breathe into this tactile connection as the two hands merge on your two hearts. Inhale together deeply from the root of the pelvis to the root of the heart for the count of 3. Pause. Exhale out from the center of your heart for the count of 3.

Repeat this 3 more times, feeling into the circuitry of connection as your two beating hearts begin to sync up.

8. Bravely blink your eyes open. Rest your eyes softly on your partner's and take the whole of this person in. Be with whatever is arising in you, whether that be laughter, discomfort, tenderness, or bodily sensations. There is nothing you need to do besides witness and be witnessed.

9. With eyes open now, return to the rhythm of your breath. As you inhale you receive love from your partner's heart and as you exhale you give love from yours. Inhale and receive love without conditions and exhale and give love without conditions. Inhale, receiving breath, life, and love and exhale, giving breath, life, and love. Feel this relationship between giving and receiving, loving and being loved, seeing and being seen, come into perfect harmony.

10. Now for the final step, we give voice to what our heart longs to speak in this moment. Keep your hridaya connection and share aloud with your partner what your heart needs to hear today.

11. Once you tell your partner what your heart needs, your partner will now offer your heart message *back to you* by speaking it aloud 3 times. For example: "You are worthy of love." "You are

enough." "I love you." After they repeat your heart message back to you 3 times, take a loving breath together and switch roles. You will become the giver, and your partner will become the receiver.

12. Once you are complete, release the connection and return your hand back to your own heart. Gently bow to one another. *Namaste*. The divine love in me sees and recognizes the divine love in you.

You can also listen to the how-to audio at www.chakrarituals.com.

Writing Contemplation

1. Take out your notebook and just write a little bit about your experience. What it felt like for you, what came up for you, what resistance was present, anything that you want to remember from this experience.

2. If you are single and want to call in your own Krishna, how can you begin to embody the qualities in yourself of what you want to attract? Make a list of these qualities. Be very clear and visualize them.

3. Complete these sentence stems.

My heart is open to _____
_____ .

Love teaches me _____
_____ .

I can see my love for myself when _____
_____ .

Having clears boundaries allows _____
_____ .

Vulnerability means to me _____
_____ .

Balance at the Heart Chakra looks like ____
_____ .

What I love most about my life is _____
_____ .

- You have two hearts, not one. The physical heart which beats and breaks and the spiritual heart that is unbreakable and never dies.

- The goddess is your ultimate dance partner, breathing you 21,000 times a day.

- Self-love is your greatest superpower.

- No one can complete you as you are already perfect, whole, and complete.

- Your heart longs to be in balance and to dance with its opposite force.

- You have a personal reservoir of limitless love that you can turn to again and again for true healing.

- Vulnerability is not weakness; it is an exquisite act of courage.

The core and the heart are intimately connected. Your diaphragm, which is a core muscle, moves downward every time you inhale. This causes the rib cage to expand and allows air to enter your lungs. When you exhale, the diaphragm contracts, rises up, and gently squeezes your heart. Think of it like a mini heart massage with each breath, the diaphragm bringing more blood flow to the most important muscle in the human body. When you are connected to your center and seated in love, it feels safe to not only breathe deeply but to speak your truth and show the world who you uniquely are! With each deepening breath, you have the opportunity to use the power of your core to bring more energy to your heart, and more truth and expression to your words!

Today is your day of reflection and rest. Take some time to reflect upon your most important takeaway from this chakra chapter. If there was only one thing you could remember from this chapter, what would it be? Maybe take a moment to note it down as we continue the journey, the one thing that you want to remember. Now is also the perfect opportunity to return back to any of the previous days' exercises or readings.

Bathe deeply in that ocean of sound
Vibrating within you, now as always,
Resonating softly,
Permeating the space of the heart.
The ear that is tuned by rapt listening
Learns to hear the song of creation.
First like a hand bell,
Then subtler, like a flute,
Subtler still as a stringed instrument,
Eventually as the buzz of a bee.
Entering this current of sound,
The Listening One,
Forget the external world, becomes
Absorbed into internal sound,
Then absorbed in vastness,
Like the song of the stars as they shine.

—THE RADIANCE SUTRAS: SUTRA 15

7

You Are Uniquely You

THE FIFTH CHAKRA

Before we go any further, I want to take a moment to pause, honor, and reflect on the path you have traveled thus far. You dove down into the depths of the great Mother Earth, tended to your roots, and bravely came home to the body. You swam through the sacred waters and gave yourself permission to feel all that you feel, arousing your desires and setting your power and passion ablaze. With confidence and courage, you ventured into the heart, and learned to love and accept yourself. With all these empowerments in hand, you are now ready to show the world who you uniquely are! As you journey up the Rainbow Path, we now enter the space of the throat

and the Vishuddhi Chakra. The Fifth Chakra and its sacred element of space is all about vibration, communication, creativity, and self-expression. *Visha* means "poison." Shuddh means "to rinse" or "to cleanse," pointing to the fact that in order to access these gifts and awaken the intelligence of the Fifth Chakra, we first must "purify the poison" that lives in our words, thoughts, and bodies. Through this process of purification, we return to what is true, honest, and authentic. We clear the pathway from the heart to the mind, and we come into divine harmony and resonance within ourselves and with the world around us.

ANATOMY OF THE CHAKRA

As we ascend the Rainbow Path, we can see the number of petals on the chakra lotus blossom from four (root), six (sacral center), eight (power center), and twelve (heart) to sixteen at the throat center. A lotus flower with sixteen petals is much more delicate and refined. This same delicacy and refinement is found in the physical tissues and structures of the neck, throat, and ears, which the Fifth Chakra governs. Inside the lotus we have a sky blue downward-pointing triangle with a white circle at the center. Here the triangle is believed to represent creativity and the path through which divine inspiration flows. The circle represents the full moon and all the intuitive blessings that it offers. The moon is a symbol of purity and the vastness of space, and it holds special significance as the sacred element of the throat. Traditionally the Vishuddhi Chakra vibrates to the color blue.

THE POWER OF SOUND AND THE SACRED ELEMENT OF SPACE

Most spiritual traditions across the world believe sound or vibration is central to the birth of the universe. Whether you listen to scientists explain the Big Bang theory, Christians testify of God speaking the world into existence, tantric yogis shout

WAYS TO CONNECT WITH AKASHA

- Go out into nature and listen to the rhythms and sounds of life.
- Spend time in silence, without your electronic devices, books, or even a journal to distract you.
- Make space in your day to connect with your spirit. Make space in your life to just be.

YOUR CHAKRA CHEAT SHEET

Name	Vishuddhi Vish (poison) Shuddhi (To wash, to cleanse, to purify)	**Bija Sound**	HAM (pronounced "hum")
Meaning	Purity and Self Expression	**Vowel Sound**	AI (pronounced "eye")
Physical Location	Throat	**Energetics**	Truth, Authenticity
Element	Akasha / Space (sound vibration)	**Affirmations**	I am unique. I am bringing to life my unique and powerful voice. I sing songs of truth. I am free to be me and express the beauty of my soul. My words matter.
Color	Blue		
Sense	Hearing		

Body parts related	Throat Vocal chords Cervical spine Ears Jaw Tongue Trachea Roof of the mouth to the top of the lungs Thyroid gland
Effects of Deficiency	Fear of speaking up Difficult time putting words into feelings Shyness, inability to express who you really are Speech impediments, stuttering, loss of voice Tightness in shoulders and throat Defensiveness, excessive judgment or criticism
Effect of Excess	Lies, gossips, talks too much Loud, dominating talker, constantly interrupts Manipulates with their words Unable to listen or hear others' perspectives
Balance	Speaks authentically from the heart Deeply listens to others Clear, direct, and thoughtful communication Honest, true, trustworthy Lives artfully Embraces and celebrates uniqueness

the great pranava *om* that sets the entire universe into motion, or others who recount the goddess Saraswati singing the universes into being, all traditions point to one feature regarding the birth of the universe: that the world was created through sound or cosmic vibration. For sound or vibration to happen, we also need something else. The etheric, invisible element of creation is Space, or *akasha* in Sanskrit. In yogic philosophy, it is akasha that gives rise to the other four elements (Air, Fire, Water, and Earth). It is the infinite field of pure potentiality from which all of creation originates, pulsates, and dances into existence. You can imagine akasha as the infinite sky, the wide-open expanse.

EXPRESS YOURSELF

You might never imagine that someone who talks for a living could be disempowered in their voice in their personal life. You might find it difficult to believe that a woman who knows one of her greatest gifts is her ability to inspire through her words, to speak with energy, passion, and poetic resonance, is the same woman who surrenders her voice to another again and again. I am this woman. In my professional life, I am a speaker, hardly ever at a loss for words, and I know I am blessed with the gift of gab! When I speak, I am connected, present, grounded, able to communicate from my heart and from my embodied wisdom. The words I

speak in my professional life land easily on the ears of listeners and touch many deeply. However, in my personal life this is not the case. I have struggled to put my feelings into words, to speak up for myself, to ask for what I need, or to call someone out when I know they are being dishonest or they do something that hurts me. My voice was so shut down that even if I was getting a massage and the masseuse was hurting me or making me feel uncomfortable, I could not muster the words to ask them to stop, ease off on the pressure, or not to touch me there. Instead, I would fall back into my highly developed pattern of detaching from my body, so I didn't have to be present with or feel the pain of what was happening. You can see how this could cause some major issues in my personal life beyond the massage table. For me, these problems with communication show up most clearly in my romantic relationships with men.

Surrendering my voice in a relationship was the equivalent of surrendering my power. For years I said yes when I wanted to say no. I did not question the mixed messages, I stayed silent when I was screaming inside, and I lacked the ability to put my true, honest feelings into words. At times I would be so full of energy that I felt like I might explode. I would practice, repeating the words in my head again and again of what I wanted to say, but when I came face-to-face with the person, I would be paralyzed with fear and end up saying nothing, or the words would come out the wrong way. Instead of coming from a place of power, my words would come from the wounded, weak, or needy place inside me, and I would be left feeling worse.

I know I am not alone in this type of Fifth Chakra collapse. I see it all over the world, in the faces of the women I teach when I share my own stories and listen to theirs. There are so many reasons why even seemingly powerful women do not or cannot speak up. Perhaps it is because you come from a culture or family where a woman's voice is not respected or valued; or maybe you were told to shut up enough times as a child that you began to believe your voice had no worth; or possibly you have suffered some kind of abuse, verbal, physical, or sexual, and you learned quickly that your silence kept you safe, even kept you alive. No matter the reason, we must learn to expunge the poison of our swallowed words from out of our system.

Years ago, I became romantically involved with someone with whom I was working. We had big plans of offering luxury yoga and wellness retreats around the world. On our first (and only) retreat, once the opening circle began, he immediately took over and positioned himself as the leader and me as his assistant. He even began to pretend that we were not romantically involved. Most if not all of the participants came from my connections, and I did all the administrative and organizational work behind the scenes to make the retreat happen. So if anyone should have been in an assistant's role, it was him! But I am embarrassed to say that *I let it happen.* I didn't fight him or argue with his behavior, I just collapsed onto myself and pretended for the weekend that everything was fine. On the last day of the retreat, I physically lost my voice (which at the time was not uncommon for me); from days (and a lifetime) of swallowing my words, my voice would be taken from me, not because I was sick, but because I didn't have the courage to speak up.

To really be able to voice your truth, you need to feel safe, secure, and grounded in your body (First Chakra); to *feel* the flow of your emotions and be able to put them into words (Second Chakra); to claim your courage and bravery to speak up (Third Chakra); and be vulnerable enough to risk being hurt and come into harmony with the highest vibration so you can speak from your heart (Fourth Chakra). If this foundation is set, the pathway to the Fifth Chakra can open and express with honesty, clarity, and conviction what is inside of you. You can really begin to see how the chakras work together to support, heal, and awaken the entire system. Each chakra, while offering its unique intelligence, is cheering on the one following to truly show up, to participate in the dance, and to play its part in empowering the whole!

RECLAIMING YOUR VOICE

Reclaiming your voice and being able to speak up, especially when the stakes feel high, is something that doesn't happen overnight. It takes daily practice to exercise the muscle of speaking up—and awareness to recognize when you are inhibited. One of the most powerful ways to do this is by starting to use your voice in a non-threatening way. Below are some of my favorite techniques that have strengthened this muscle for me both physically and energetically. The bare simplicity and fun of these exercises will release you into their full accessible potency and potential to find your VOICE! Singing, dancing, and chanting have persisted for millennia in one form or another in every culture around the globe! One more thing before we get started: you CAN sing, and you CAN dance. This comes from my dear soul sister Daphne Tse, an internationally acclaimed singer, songwriter, yogini, and teacher, who has the voice of an angel. Through her work she taught me that our voice is medicine, and our body is the instrument for expression and joy. She reminds me again and again to fall in love with the sound of my own voice, to sing from the heart, and to share my song with the world.

1. *SINGING*: Put on your favorite song and sing it at the top of your lungs in your living room, shower, or car. Act out the song and bring your full expression into the words and your movements. Try putting on the YouTube videos of songs to sing and dance along!

2. *CHANTING*: You can think of chanting as singing your prayers! Traditionally it is done in Sanskrit, as it is a vibratory language that is believed to awaken consciousness. You can imagine the words as spiritual sound formulas designed to land on the body and tune it in a very specific way. I am in love with this energy language and all its hidden depths, but just because I am does not mean you have to be as well. Know you always have full permission to chant or sing in whatever language that you like. We have already explored a number of mantras in both Sanskrit and English from *aum, klim, shrim, mana mandire, aham prema*, to *This is my body, I thank you, and I release you,* and *I am the goddess, I am the warrior!* You can play with any of these or any other words or mantras you already know that resonate in your heart and body. The gift of chanting mantras (a tool to protect the mind, purify the voice, and bridge the gap between the heart and the head) comes through our own intentionality and repetition. Through this process, you fortify and strengthen the energetic

field of your voice and heart and sing the blessing of your mantra to life. You are raising not only your vibration but the vibration of the space you are in. You will get to explore the power of chanting the chakra sounds in the ritual section of this chapter.

3. *Shake, Rattle, and Roar!* I am a BIG fan of shaking (hence why you have been practicing some form of it within previous chakra exercises), as it is the perfect antidote for your inhibitions. It is fun, freeing, and moves out the heavy, stuck, and congested energy. Couple shaking with sound and get ready to blast off and awaken your wild woman within! The best part is, shaking is fast—really fast. It takes just two minutes to recalibrate your entire energy field and open up the flow of prana through your Throat Chakra and the entire body. *Shake, rattle, and roar* is an invitation to play, to systematically shake and wake each part of the body, while giving each part a voice (using nonsensical sounds). Try starting with the wrists and hands. As you shake them vigorously, ask them what kind of sound they want to make today and open your mouth and make it. Really go for it, open your mouth wide, and let your expression out. Continue on to your shoulders, heart, belly, booty, legs, feet, and even your head, asking each part what kind of sounds it wants

to make. The movement and the sound work together to release the old stories, unsaid words, and stagnant energy held in your tissues. Free them now and give them a voice. After you feel complete, take a moment to ground your body and take several deep breaths. Notice how alive you are as vibration courses through your body. Without judgment, take note of which parts of the body held the biggest and the smallest shakes and sounds. Are there any areas of the body you resisted moving or expressing outward through sound? Where did you feel the most free?

4. In this last technique, we switch from *making sound* to *deeply listening.* It can be done on its own or after a *chanting* or *shake, rattle, and roar* practice. I suggest coming into a comfortable, grounded, seated position and closing your eyes to the degree that is comfortable to you. As you go inside, start to connect with your feeling body and ask, *Why don't you speak up?* or *What is it you really want to say?* Then simply make space to listen for an answer to arise. Be super compassionate with yourself and do not judge or invalidate any answer you receive. The body holds great wisdom and remembers even when the mind forgets. When we give our body the space and the permission to speak, we have the opportunity to give voice to our wounds

and our light. We strengthen our skills of listening. When you access the part of the psyche that holds the vibration of truth, the answers you receive will be much more eloquent and profound than those received by the mind. If a lot is coming up for you, this could be excellent work to do with a therapist or somatic healer.

CREATIVITY RECOVERY: ERNIE'S BIG MESS

Another beautiful empowerment of the Throat Chakra is the embrace of creativity. According to renowned teacher, author, and artist Julia Cameron, who has unleashed the creative flow in millions of people around the world, creativity is not something you do—it is something that you are. Julia teaches that the creative process is a way of engaging with the god, goddess, spirit, or higher consciousness. That there is no higher act. That creativity is your gift from God and what you create is your gift back to God.

Now if this sounds too woo-woo to you, maybe you would like to hear what science has to say on the subject. Researchers like Scott Barry Kaufman who study the science of creativity and imagination discovered that we are biologically hardwired to create. That we are creative beings by nature and that we are happiest and healthiest when we are creating. Since creativity is our birthright and what we were literally born to do, instead of learning to be creative, we have to unlearn all the ways we are told we are not! We all have creative injuries to overcome and blocks to dissolve or dismantle. My own road to creativity recovery took me back to when I was six years old and in the first grade at Visitation Academy in Brooklyn, New York. We were given the assignment of doing our first book report, a one-page report with a cover. I picked the book *Ernie's Big Mess*, as I was a big fan of *Sesame Street*. I wrote the report and pulled out my construction paper, crayons, and markers and got to work. I created what I thought was a masterpiece. Proudly, I showed it to my mother, and she said, "Why don't I help you with this?" The next day I arrived at school, and I knew I had the best cover, as my mom, instead of helping me, completely redid mine. It was so good that it rivaled the cover of the actual book! The day I was praised for being a great artist was the same day I stopped drawing and shut down my inner artist. From that moment on my mother did every art project of mine. But one day in fifth grade, our class was assigned an *in*-class project. Each person was given a specific role to contribute to the project. I was chosen to do the drawing, because I was the best! My heart started to race as I had no idea what I was going to do; I could not handle the embarrassment of my secret being revealed. I raised my hand and asked to go to the bathroom, and the bathroom is where I stayed. I stayed so long that one of the other

students was sent to check on me. When I returned to the class, I told the teacher I just threw up and I was sent home. I narrowly escaped my "lie" of being a great artist.

Almost twenty years later, I was haunted by this incident once again. One of my closest friends was having an art party for his birthday. A dozen friends, five canvases, and all the paints, brushes, scrapers, and sponges you could ever want came together to create the art for his new apartment. I knew this time there was no escape, that he was my best friend, and that I certainly couldn't hide in the bathroom *again.* I had to face the terror (I know it might sound strange, but it really was terrifying for me) and the embarrassment of being so truly bad at art that I might ruin his paintings. No pressure—at least this time the "class" did not think I was going to be the next Georgia O'Keeffe. Brush in hand, all I could think about was little Cristi with the brown construction paper and red marker, smiling. This ended up being one of the most healing days for my inner artist to step above my inner perfectionist. Once I was able to give myself permission to let the six-year-old Cristi make a glorious mess, I was liberated. And I had so much fun! I realized how much of my creative spirit had been on lockdown because of the false beliefs that I had held: **1)** I was not an artist, **2)** it was not okay to be a beginner at anything, and **3)** it was not okay to create something just for the joy of it, even and especially if you aren't good at it!

This day was truly the start of me reclaiming my creative life.

I am still no Georgia (just in case you were wondering), but through the lens by which I now view creativity, I do see my life as a work of art. I consider myself an artist of movement, of yoga, and of dance. I see artistry in the musical soundscapes I create for my classes, in the words I speak when I teach, and the words I write in the pages of this book. Creating art is how I express myself, move through my pent-up emotions, and even meditate. Next time you are stuck in your head, try pulling out some crayons, paper, vinyls, or whatever creative medium you like. Set a timer for 20 minutes and see what emerges through you as you commune with the creative impulse and give yourself permission to make a beautiful mess. My hope for you is that whether it's through writing, music, fashion, or decor, you recognize that you too are an artist, working on the most important creation of all: your life. The embodiment ritual at the end of this chapter will inspire and reawaken the artist that is you.

SHE WHO FLOWS: MEET THE GODDESS SARASWATI

To support the full flowering of the Vishuddhi Chakra we turn to the great goddess who is said to live on the tip of the poet's tongue, in the stroke of the painter's brush, and in the flourish of the composer's score. Meet Saraswati, the ruling deity of the arts, and the goddess of speech, articulation, creativity, intuition, and knowledge. Her name means "the flowing one," as she is the sacred flow of ideas, insight, and divine inspiration. She is the goddess of authentic expression who invites you to sing your song, dance your dance, tell your story, and share your unique essence with the world.

Saraswati is traditionally depicted as riding astride a white swan and softly strumming the Indian stringed instrument called the veena. She holds a *mala*, or string of prayer beads, in one hand and a book of spiritual wisdom in the other. Her swan, or *hamsa* in Sanskrit, is a symbol of purity and liberation. It has the gift of discerning truth, just as it can separate milk from water so Saraswati only receives what is nourishing. Her veena has seven strings, each string representing one of the seven chakras. She is playing us, fine-tuning our unique frequency to bring us into our highest vibration. Her prayer beads speak to the power of mantra and to one of her great mythic stories of singing the world into manifestation. The book she holds is the most ancient of all the yogic texts, the Vedas. Saraswati is an independent goddess, who doesn't care much for domestication. She would rather spend her days creating, learning, studying, and embodying deeper wisdom and truths than being someone's wife. Her colors are white, blue, and yellow,

and she is luminous like full moonlight.

Saraswati is the goddess I turn to when initiating creative projects. I make offerings to her daily in the form of song, dance, and flowers, and I even create altars in her honor. I carry her picture with me and chant her mantra, *aum aim saraswatyai namaha*. I ask her to be the ink in my pen, to be the clarity of my voice, and to be the inspiration that flows through me.

Where in your life do you need the divine blessing of Saraswati? Maybe you need help speaking up or finding your voice, or maybe you are embarking on some creative project or a path of higher learning. Let's together invoke her name by repeating her mantra nine times. Allow her vibration into your entire being with her shakti, her energy, of inspiration.

aum aim saraswatyai namaha

aum ("ohm"): The great pranava, the primordial sound of creation

aim ("eye-im"): The seed mantra for the great shakti power of creative inspiration, knowledge, and the spoken word.

saraswatayai ("suh-ruh-swah-tie-yeh")

namaha ("nuh-muh-huh"): A bow of reverence to the feminine shakti

YOUR UNIQUE FREQUENCY

Over fifteen years ago, I had the opportunity to study with an Indian teacher/guru. I participated in many of his courses, my favorite being a Chakra Energization course. In this offering, when talking about the Vishuddhi Chakra, he said that the way in which the sixteen lotus petals blossom open is through celebrating and honoring our uniqueness and our creativity. He said each person is born with a highly individualized, highly distinctive energy frequency or signature, and encoded in this signature are the unique gifts that only you possess. Similar to your fingerprint, no two are alike. This signature is what makes you, uniquely you. When you are *in tune* with this frequency, you are in your most authentic power and truth. You are in harmony with your inner world—all five elements (Earth, Water, Fire, Air, and Space) and seven chakras are celebrating, singing, dancing, having a party inside of you. When this happens, you are able to communicate from the heart with clarity and wisdom, and your words land, hold resonance, and make an impact. You are aligned to your highest expression; able to shine, go after your dreams, and be and express who you truly are.

However, this frequency can get frayed when you don't honor and appreciate who you are. When you worry about what others think or get caught in jealousy and comparison, there is temptation to start writing checks forging another's (energy) signature. No matter how good your skills of forgery become, you will always be *out of tune,* out of harmony with yourself, disconnected from the people around you and the universe.

The following six practices are here to help you connect with the essence of your unique frequency and activate the power of your Vishuddhi Chakra.

THE PRACTICES: 7 DAYS OF EXPRESSION

Day One: Altar

Your Altar of Expression is the place you will come every day to do your Vishuddhi Chakra rituals. Let this creation be an opportunity to bring what is inside of you out. Get creative. And give yourself permission to express yourself through color, textures, images, symbols, objects, words, and sounds. Allow the mere sight of your altar to serve as a dose of inspiration and to remind you of your uniqueness.

Start with the essentials and then build from there.

Altar Essentials

- Something blue (cloth, candle, crystal, paper)
- Something that represents the element of space or sound (singing bowls, chimes, rattle, a bell, or play your favorite song)
- An item that represents creative expression (a journal, sketch pad, paints, musical instrument, dance shoes)

Altar Inspirations

- Something to burn: white sage, palo santo, piñon, incense
- Image of Saraswati
- Words or affirmations, either written or painted
- Crystals: aquamarine, apatite, chrysocolla
- Oils: lavender, Valor, cypress
- Tarot Cards: The Justice, The Moon, Ace of Fire

Refer to the Quick Charts in the Appendix for extended meanings of crystals, oils, and tarot cards.

Writing Contemplation

1. What is your relationship to the element of Space? What does it mean to be spacious with yourself? How can you create more space in your body, your mind, and your life? How will this spaciousness support you? And, most importantly, what are you creating space for?

2. Recall that the meaning of Vishuddhi is to purify the poison. What poison or toxicity lives in your system and environment, and how can you purify yourself of it? Examine your body, thoughts, speech, relationships, diet, and even your home.

3. How would you define healthy communication? Are you able to freely and clearly communicate your truth and your needs? Are there any miscommunications or misunderstandings that need to be addressed and healed—from the words you either spoke or failed to speak? How have you misused your voice? Are you willing to take responsibility for the power and impact of your words and voice?

Day Two: Mudra—Matangi

The mudra we are practicing today is called matangi mudra. Matangi is one of the ten great tantric wisdom goddesses. Her name means "thought," "knowledge," or "the spoken word," and she is said to reside in the center of the throat. She is the power of *vac*, the Sanskrit word for the potency of our voice and the words we speak. She purifies our vibrations, thoughts, words, and expressions. Practicing her mudra helps to clear the pathway from the head to the heart, a difficult juncture for many of us to cross. She opens us up to conscious communication—a combination of both speaking and listening—and thereby to truth and inspiration.

Here are the step-by-step instructions.

1. Find a comfortable seat in front of your altar. Sit up tall, and ground into your pelvis.

2. Bring your hands into anjali (prayer) mudra at your heart and take 3 deep breaths.

3. Interlace all ten of your fingers.

4. Extend your middle fingers up to the sky. The middle finger represents the element of space, Akasha, the sacred element of the Throat Chakra. It also represents the integrated self, creative freedom, and expression.

5. Create a seal between your thumb (fire) and first finger (air).

6. Take the shape to the base of your solar plexus. If you feel comfortable doing so, close your eyes.

7. Take 5 slow, deep, *nourishing breaths*. Imagine a beautiful blue light blazing upward from your solar plexus, through the heart, throat, and up to your third eye center. This is the light of truth, the light of clarity, purifying any toxicity or lies that live in your system.

8. Maintain the mudra and extend your arms overhead. Ground down into your pelvis again and sit tall in your spine. Breathe into this radiant channel that roots you to the earth and extends you up in the direction of deep space—pure potentiality and inspiration.

9. Unhinge your jaw; soften the muscles of your face and neck. Sense your ears opening and the space of your throat expanding.

10. Take 5 more deep breaths.

11. Feel the radiance and luminosity in your throat.

12. Once you feel complete, open your eyes and release the mudra. Pause and notice how open and spacious your Throat Chakra feels.

You can also listen to the how-to audio at www.chakrarituals.com.

This is a mudra I personally use before I teach a big class, make a presentation, or have to have a difficult conversation. Especially in stressful situations, it acts as a tuning fork to align heart and mind with the divine. With the heart and mind unified in purpose, we can speak with greater clarity, authenticity, and conviction.

Writing Contemplation

1. One writing prompt that I work with when my voice gets shut down and I get lost for words is: *What I really want to say is . . .* Try writing it over and over again on a piece of paper until something comes out the other side.

2. Think about a specific situation in which you were not able to speak up. Did your silence help the situation or make matters worse? How did remaining silent make you feel? Can you return to this moment in your mind's eye now? If there was no harmful consequence, what are the words you would speak and to whom? Hear yourself saying them now as you are writing them down. Leave nothing out. Once you are complete, take a few deep breaths and notice how you feel.

3. The Fifth Chakra is not just about how we speak to others, it is also about how we speak to ourselves. What are the mantras running on repeat in your head? Do they sound something like, *I am so AMAZING, I am inherently worthy,* or *I am so Powerful*? Or do they sound more like, *I am so stupid, I don't deserve my dream job,* or *I am worthless*? Be honest when you are making your list. Next to each "negative" mantra create a new positive statement. Anytime throughout the week when you catch yourself reinforcing your negative mantra, immediately replace the thought with your new positive statement. What you practice you strengthen, and what you strengthen you take on as truth!

The pranayama technique we are practicing for the Vishuddhi Chakra is one of my favorites and is known as *Simhasana,* or lion's breath. Lion's breath helps to clear out any of the stuck or stagnated energy that is held in the chest, lungs, and throat. Anything that is blocking your creative expression, your ability to speak, or your ownership of your own voice. It also stretches the muscles of the face, the jaw, and the neck, alleviating hidden tension or stress trapped there.

Get ready to drop your inhibitions, because you are going to open your mouth wide, let your tongue unfurl, turn your eyes upward, and roar like the lioness that you are!

Let's get started.

1. Find a comfortable, grounded seat. Hands rest on your knees or thighs.

2. Take three deep breaths, inhaling through your nose and exhaling out through the nose.

3. Inhale in through your nose. Exhale, open your mouth, stretch your tongue out, roll your eyes up to the brow center, and ROAR!

4. Rinse and repeat: Inhale through the nose. Exhale, stretch your tongue out as far as you can, roll your eyes up, and make some noise!

5. Try it 3–5 more times.

6. After the last one, sit for a moment and feel the effects. Notice the freedom this breath elicits, along with the invitation to be and express the wild woman that you are.

You can also listen to the how-to audio at www.chakrarituals.com.

NOTE: Another fun way to play with Simhasana that is sure to make you feel extra lionessy is to sit on your feet for the inhale and then exhale into tabletop position as you roar!

Do not be alarmed if you begin to cough, it just means you are clearing out excess congestion from your system.

Don't be afraid to make some sound. The sound is liberating in two ways: it helps to move the stuck energy out of your body, and it shakes you free of conforming to a domestic self. All the words you have swallowed, everything you have held inside. Now is the time to start to move it out. Give yourself permission to truly embody the lioness and ROAR!

Writing Contemplation

1. How and to whom in your life are you speaking your truth? How and to whom are you not? How would speaking or expressing your truth make you feel?

2. We all need a place in which we can truly express ourselves uncensored, with radical freedom and honesty. For me this happens in the pages of my journal and on the dance floor. This is how I release all I am holding inside and come more fully alive. What are your favorite outlets for expression? What makes you feel most alive?

3. What stops you from being authentically yourself?

Day Four: Vishuddhi Body Prayer

Welcome to day four, your body prayer for your Throat Chakra. This shakti-infused salutation will open up new creative pathways of movement and expression, freeing your neck, shoulders, and even your inhibitions and giving rise to what in Sanskrit is called *sahaja*, the spontaneous pulsation, or dance of life.

Suggested use: Repeat the sequence 1 to 3 times leading on each side. Follow the pictures to come or watch the how-to video at www.chakrarituals.com.

Start standing, feet hip-width apart, knees soft.

1. Inhale; lift your head and stretch your throat. Exhale; wave down through your spine. Inhale; tone belly and roll up to standing. Repeat 3 more times

2. Step your right foot back into low lunge

3. Lower your right knee to the ground. Right hand to right hip. Left arm sweeps up and circles across the body

4. Left hand to support and lengthen sacrum while right hand cradles and tractions the base of the skull

5. Hands down, step back to high plank. Exhale; lower your knees, chest, and chin to the ground

6. Sahaja cobra. Sway your torso, shoulders, head, and neck from side to side as you inhale and slowly rise up and exhale to lower down

7. Push back to child's pose

8. Roll up and sit on your heels, tent your fingers behind you, lift your chest, and stretch your throat open

9. Rise up onto knees. Place left hand to support and lengthen sacrum, right hand cradles and tractions the base of the skull. Curl up and back to open chest and throat

10. Sit down on your heels, and bring your hands to prayer at your heart. Take a full breath in and out

11. Press back to downward-facing dog

12. Step to the top of the mat, roll up to standing, hands to prayer at your heart

Repeat on the second side, stepping back with your left foot.

Writing Contemplation

1. When we tell a lie, slander, or gossip about another, we come out of resonance with ourself, and our energetic field gets damaged. Even if no one else ever finds out what you said or that you lied, YOU will always know the truth. For the next week pay attention to (or better yet write down in your journal or in your phone) every time you tell a lie or offer "alternative facts." Include every single one, no matter how small or large. This includes the lies you tell yourself. At the end of the week, review the list and ask yourself what was so wrong with the truth that you had to lie.

2. What is your *Ernie's Big Mess*? Where and when was your creative expression or artistry shut down? Maybe you were told a dancer's life was no life for you or that your poetry wasn't good enough, your voice was just mediocre, and no one would ever buy your art. Are you ready and willing to begin the road to your own creative recovery?

3. Saraswati is the goddess of the arts, creativity, knowledge, and intuition. How do you relate to her? Where in your life would you like to bring her blessings and empowerments?

Day Five: Meditation—The Power of HUM

The sound of your own voice is a healing medicine for your mind, body, and soul. In today's meditation, we will explore the power of this medicine through chanting the chakra sound for your center of expression. If you recall from chapter 1, each chakra has what is called a bija mantra or sound. *Bija* is the Sanskrit word for "seed," and it is said that the seed sound carries the full intelligence and full empowerment of the chakra. By chanting the seed sound for the throat, *HAM* (pronounced "hum"), you create a vibrational vortex that clears, awakens, and attunes the chakra and unlocks the power of your voice.

We are going to play with making the sound in three distinct ways: 1) out loud, 2) as a whisper, and 3) silently in your mind. When making the sound, allow it to vibrate as loud and as long as you can on the exhalation without straining. Simply focus on the vibration permeating through the whole of your Throat Chakra—neck, shoulders, throat, jaw, ears, mouth, and tongue. After the final round, you will have time to dissolve into the spaciousness of the sound vibration.

As I shared earlier, chanting and sounding practices were instrumental in the recovery of my own voice as they helped me harness the energy and the strength to begin speaking up. When you first begin chanting or sounding practices, you may feel wildly uncomfortable, embarrassed even. I know I did! This is part of it; face the discomfort, drop your inhibitions, don't worry what someone else might think, have fun, and fall in love with the sound of your voice. As you do this, you will attune yourself to your highest frequency so you can more easily vibrate out your authentic truth.

Here are the instructions for your meditation.

1. Come to a comfortable seated position at your altar. Ground down into the earth through your pelvis and rise up tall through your spine.

2. Take three deep breaths, inhaling through your nose and exhaling through your mouth with an audible sigh.

3. Inhale from the roots of earth into your throat; exhale out through your Vishuddhi Chakra.

4. Inhale into your center of expression; exhale out the sound *ham* ("hummmmmmmmm"). Feel the vibration filling the front, back, and sides of the throat, purifying your internal words and thoughts. Repeat 6 more times.

5. Now, take the sound to a whisper and repeat 7 times.

6. Lastly, bring the sound inside. Vibrate *ham* silently within your body and mind 7 more times, inhaling deeply and exhaling out *hummmmmmmmm.*

7. Dissolve into the spaciousness of the sound. Allow the vibrations to settle. Bathe yourself in the exquisite space of silence for the next 5 minutes. Let it wash over you.

8. When you feel complete, breathe once again from the roots of earth into your throat center; and exhale out through your Vishuddhi Chakra.

You can also listen to the how-to audio at www.chakrarituals.com.

Writing Contemplation

1. Take a few moments to reflect upon the sound meditation. What differences did you notice from chanting the sounds out loud, versus as a whisper or internally? Did you prefer one or the other? Did the sound delight or excite you? Can you describe what you felt?

2. What do you most need to hear today? Don't overthink it; trust the first thing that comes to mind. Perhaps it is *I am enough just as I am,* or *I've got this,* or *I love you.* Once you have your message, go to a mirror and look yourself in the eye; repeat your message to yourself out loud three times. Allow yourself to fully receive the vibration and resonance of your words.

3. The Greek philosopher Zeno said we have two ears and only one mouth, so that we can listen twice as much as we speak. How well do you listen, and how

can you be more present to fully listen? Are you able to hear other people's perspectives even if they are different than your own? What are you not hearing?

Day Six: Embodiment—Take Your Inner Artist on a Date

The artist date is an essential part of cultivating the creative self, and it comes from the work of Julia Cameron and her famous book *The Artist's Way*. The first time I read Cameron's book, I was in my twenties. I didn't see myself as a creative person or as an *art*ist at the time, as I could not draw, paint, sing, or write poetry, all the things that first come to mind when we initially think of the word *art*ist. One of the most powerful lessons Julia Cameron's work taught me was that creativity is not something you do; it is who you are. You are creating *art*istry with every word you speak, story you tell, and dance you dance. The way you wear your makeup, fix your hair, get dressed, or prep your food—all are reflections of the *art*ist you are. To inspire your own creative awakening, this week you are going to take yourself on an *art*ist *date*.

Taking yourself on an *art*ist date is a way of scheduling some *play* into your life and reclaiming your own creative life. You can source inspiration for your date from the things you loved doing as a little girl. Did you love to color, paint, sing, dance, play dress-up, build forts or castles? Or what are the things that for years you have been telling your friends you really want to try that you have never made time for? Now is the time!

A few date guidelines:

1. Make it a solo expedition.

2. Little or no cost.

3. Nothing that involves your "to-do list"—This is your time to PLAY!

4. Internal resistance might show up and tell you this is silly or stupid. Do not listen to this voice; it will only keep you blocked.

5. The key element is FUN, not perfection! Be willing to suck and be a beginner.

Julia says the artist date contains the potency to "uncork your creativity, sharpen your intuition, and even get you laid!"[1] Be as creative as you like, but remember this is a solo expedition, just between you and your inner artist. Some of my favorite artist dates and suggestions:

Take a movement class outside of your norm—belly dancing, hip-hop, hula hoop, pilates, salsa.

Go to the theatre and see a play or dance performance.

Finger paint.

Go to a museum.

Draw in the sand.

Take a singing lesson.

Buy and play a musical instrument.

Spend the day naked.

Write a poem or a song.

Writing Contemplation

1. Write about your artist date. Did you have resistance around planning or taking your artist date? Did you enjoy the date? Is this a ritual you could bring into your weekly life?

2. Make a list of five more artist dates you would like to go on.

3. Make a list of at least five of your unique attributes, your gifts.

Day Seven: Lessons from Your Chakra of Expression

- Your words, your voice, your truth matters!

- Four ways to reclaim your voice: sing, chant, shimmy shake, and listen deeply.

- Mantras can be sung or spoken in ANY language out loud, as a whisper, or quietly within.

- Creativity is your birthright and it's okay to be a beginner.

- Your life is a work of art.

- Your inner artist deserves to be courted—take her out on a weekly date!

- The world needs the unique medicine that only you have to offer!

As you ascend from the Vishuddhi Chakra, at the throat, to the Ajna Chakra, at the third eye, you carry with you the embodied wisdom of the sacred five elements and the intelligence of the first five chakras. With the pathway now clear from your heart to your mind, you are ready to enter into the realms of the magical and the mystical. Get ready to deepen your exploration into play and into your dreams and to awaken your imagination and intuition.

Today is your day of reflection and rest. Take some time to reflect upon your most important takeaway from this chakra chapter. If there was only one thing you could remember from this chapter, what would it be? Maybe take a moment to note it down as we continue the journey, the one thing that you want to remember. Now is also the perfect opportunity to return back to any of the previous days' exercises or readings.

Inside the skull there is a place
Where the essences of creations play and mingle—
The ecstatic light of awareness
And the awareness of that light.
The divine feminine and masculine
Sport with one another in that place
The light of their love-play illumines all space.
Rest in that light
Ever present, and gradually
Awaken into the steady joy of
That which is always everywhere.

—The Radiance Sutras: Sutra 11

8

You Are Magic

THE SIXTH CHAKRA

We've all heard of the "third eye," but few people actually know how to activate its power. The Sixth Chakra—the Ajna Chakra—is the command center of our intuition and the seat of our deepest wisdom. It is located at the brow center in the middle of the forehead. At this point in our journey, we have moved beyond the physical and the tangible into the realms of the mental, magical, and mystical. Sadly, many of us have lost access to these realms and/or belief in their existence. Society tells us that the world of daydreams, wonderment, color, and imaginary friends should be left to children. We are taught that we must grow up, get real, become serious, and trust only objective thought, only what we can see and touch. The Ajna doorway is an invitation to see a different reality, one that inspires us to once again dream, manifest, and use our imagination in new and playful ways. When we dissect the word *imagination,* we find *magi,* which means "magician." When we gain full access to our intuitive power, it ignites a spark of magic that empowers you to listen within, trust your instincts, and manifest the life of your dreams.

ANATOMY OF THE CHAKRA

The yantra for the Ajna Chakra is depicted as a lotus flower with two petals. The petals represent the dance of duality that dissolves into oneness at the brow center. One petal represents Shiva and the light of the sun, while the second petal represents Shakti and the illumination of moonlight. Brilliant rays of light emanate from each petal in opposite directions. One petal directs its light downward, filling the lower chakras all the way to the earth, while the other shines upward through the crown of the head and up into the heavens.[1] Within the lotus flower there is a downward-pointing triangle (as we have seen in the yantras for the First, Third, Fourth, and Fifth Chakras) symbolizing the feminine creative energy of shakti and the path of manifestation. Within the triangle we find the sonic form of creation, the great pranava, OM. The Ajna Chakra vibrates and spins at the color indigo.

INNER ILLUMINATION

Traditionally there are only five sacred elements (Earth, Water, Fire, Air, and Space) so at the level of the third eye, some chakra systems suggest we are beyond an element, just like we are beyond the body at this part in the journey. Anodea Judith, author, therapist, and one of the great wisdom keepers of the chakra system, offers another perspective and says *Light* is the element of the Sixth Chakra. I like to think about it this way. The eyes are the windows to our outer and inner worlds. It is through the power of *Light* that we can see through these windows.

WAYS TO CONNECT WITH THE LIGHT

- Honor the rhythms of daily light, getting up early to watch the sunrise.

- Watch the sun set and the moon rise into the night sky.

- Bathe in the moonlight and under the stars.

- Don't take yourself too seriously, keep an element of *Lightness.*

- Play with the darkness: rub your palms together vigorously for thirty seconds (fire kindling mudra), then cup your hands over your eyes, bathing them in the warmth of the darkness. Take several deep breaths in and out.

- Try some simple yoga asana with your eyes closed. Tadasana, Warrior 2, Goddess; if you are feeling brave, Tree pose. Rely on your inner site, your inner light of awareness.

- Follow the ritual practices in this chapter.

YOUR CHAKRA CHEAT SHEET

Name	Ajna	**Bija Sound**	OM	
Meaning	Command, Inner Illumination, Unlimited Power	**Vowel Sound**	NG	
Physical Location	Brow Center	**Energetics**	Insight and creating a vision	
Element	Light	**Affirmations**	I see. I am envisioning . . . I am guided. I AM Magic. I expand my scope of vision beyond what is possible. Today I am creating a better version of myself. I am open to my highest awareness and guidance.	
Color	Indigo or Purple			
Sense	Sixth sense			

Body parts related	Forehead, eyes, brain, nervous system
Effects of Deficiency	Lack of imagination, creativity, and inspiration Disconnection from inner guidance Denial (can't see what is really going on) Inability to think outside the box or to see alternatives Overly serious, excessively intellectual Unable to self reflect Has difficulty manifesting one's visions or dreams
Effects of Excess	Disconnected from reality, paranoid, excessive fantasizing Nightmares Intrusive memories Difficulty concentrating, lack of clarity
Balance	Trusts and is guided by intution Clear insight Creative imagination Increased dreams (literally and figuratively) Open-minded Able to manifest your visions into reality Believes in the magic and the mystery of the universe

If you recall from chapter 1, there are three primary nadis, or rivers of light, that coalesce at the Ajna center: pingala, ida, and sushumna. Pingala governs the right side of the body, the enegy of the masculine, and the light of the sun; the ida governs the left side of the body, the energy of the feminine, and the light of the moon. The sushumna, the radiant channel, or channel of God, runs from the base of the pelvis to the crown of the head and passes through each of the seven chakras. Ida and pingala spiral around the sushumna, crisscrossing above and below each of the lower chakras. See image below.

As these three nadis dissolve into one, the mystical eye of empowerment opens and our vision is expanded to see the visible and the invisible, the seen and the unseen, inside and out. This is no ordinary vision but what I call our cosmic vision. When our cosmic vision turns on, we are able to see what we have not been able to see before, our minds expand, and the impossible becomes possible.

A WHOLE NEW WORD

The first time I went to Burning Man was the summer of 2014. More of my friends were "burners" than not, but due to work I was never able to make the trip to the infamous "Playa." I had just quit my job and was in the midst of a huge life transformation, so it was the perfect time to head to Black Rock City, Nevada, with six friends. For years I had heard countless stories, seen pictures, and even watched Burning Man documentaries, but nothing could have mentally prepared me for this experience. The first three days I was there all I could say was, "Where in the FUCK am I?" My mind literally could not grasp this alternate universe that I had arrived in nor apparently expand fast enough to catch up with it. The only explanations my thinking mind could come up with were—*I am on another planet, on a movie set,* or *I am dreaming!*

For those of you not familiar with Burning Man, it is hands down the most intentional—and the wildest— soul-fulfilling, imagination-stretching community gathering on planet Earth. For nine days, approximately 70,000 people come together to build a temporary metropolis in the barren Nevada desert known as Black Rock City. The city is constructed on a prehistoric lake bed, with ground that is likened more to flour than dirt, which certainly contributes to its otherworldly feel—it looks like what you would imagine the surface of the moon to look like. The ethos of Burning Man is built upon ten guiding principles, including radical self-expression, radical self-reliance, a gifting economy (meaning no one is paid and money does not get exchanged; your currency is a gift you offer to people), and leave no trace behind (everything you bring into the city you take out). When you arrive at the gates you are Welcomed Home, as to burners the Playa is the "Real World" and life off the Playa is the "Default World."

This Real World is like putting on your magical chakra-colored glasses and having the limited constructs of your mind shattered and your scope of vision of what is possible expanded to the boundless. We can liken this metaphor to the Ajna Chakra and imagine the "Default World" to be the world in which we only see through our two eyes. This is a world in which we too easily get stuck in the judgmental, conditioned mind that is fixated on the flawed, unable to see outside the box or beyond a black and white binary reality. This *default* reality buys into the illusion that there is no such thing as magic and that you have to see something to believe it. It is often a world filled with pain, criticism, and unworthiness. The Real World is one in which all three eyes are awakened. This is a world that is filled with color, possibility, daydreams, and magic. All three eyes are softly focused on beauty, truth, love, and curiosity.

The invitation at Burning Man and in our own lives is to frolic, to dream, to explore once again with childlike wonderment, and be in awe of all of creation. My first day at the Burn, I stumbled between an erect twenty-foot penis statue, an exquisite temple that rivaled the beauty of any I had seen around the world, and a giant boom box on wheels with my favorite DJ Marques Wyatt inside the "tape deck" spinning, while others danced freely on top.

The magic of Burning Man is not just what the expanded eye can see but comes from your full participation in being part of the very creation. It requires you not only to dream and envision but to also take action. You are responsible for playing your part in the building and/or breaking down of your respective camp and participating in the gifting economy. Our camp built a yoga deck, and we offered yoga classes twice a day as our "gift" to the community.

Burning Man is not something that can be explained, it has to be experienced, just like your intuition, your imagination, your sixth sense. As the Ajna doorway opens, you are welcomed home into the world of boundless possibilities and magic, just like Burning Man.

GIFTS FROM AN AWAKENED THIRD EYE

Intuition is a powerful *gift* that serves as an inner GPS to support the direction of our life, every step of the way. This gift is not some magical blessing that has been bestowed upon a select few, it is a boon that has been granted to all. But in order to unwrap this gift and access its magic, you first must develop an intimate relationship with it. Without this very important step, your intuition will remain but a buried treasure. In this next section, we are going to explore what intuition is, what it feels like, and the steps you can take to build, hone, and strengthen your relationship with the *gift* of your intuitive guidance.

According to my teacher and mentor Dr. Lorin Roche, intuition is our most natural state and feels like *play*. He actually compares the feeling to the glee and absolute giddiness of puppies playing. You know the state that makes you giggle, that surprises and inspires you: that is what intuition should feel like. Your intuition, just like a puppy, is always vying for and trying to get your attention. It might start off as a little nuzzle that turns into a lick, that becomes a bark, and before long turns into a pounce. By that point the puppy has already peed and maybe even pooped on your carpet, and you've missed your intuitive message or received it too late!

Let's look at five ways in which we can avoid this unnecessary cleanup and start to actively engage and forge a deeply intimate relationship with our intuition. But before we get to that, let's quickly talk about what intuition is not. Intuition should not feel like fear, anxiety, or obsessive thinking. Nor should it feel heavy or exhausting or cause the mind to spin in an endless loop. These are signs that your system is overloaded and needs a reboot. Luckily, you have access to the ritual practices at the end of the chapter that will help refresh your overloaded system. For this, I suggest you start with body prayer and then move to the breathing exercises.

1. **Make Time and Space**

   Building a relationship with your intuition is no different than building a relationship with a person. First, you must be willing to make time and space in your life. Time and space are an important part of what nurtures a relationship—how you truly get to know someone and how you begin to build trust and comfort. The best way I know how to do this with your intuition is through a daily meditation practice. You can imagine each session as a *date* with your inner guidance, as a time to dial in and intimately engage with what is inside. Knowingly or unknowingly, you have already been *dating* your inner self for the last six weeks! As you have been carving out time and space to do all the daily empowerment practices—your energetic system is now primed to meet your inner guidance. The meditation at the end of this chapter will take this to the next level.

2. Awareness: Pay Attention and Listen

Now that you have committed to showing up for your inner guidance, it is time to learn how it prefers to communicate with you. Your intuition may choose to speak to you in the form of a *bodily sensation*—think goosebumps on your skin, the hair on the back of your neck standing up, that feeling of *oh yes* or *oh no* in your gut, or even your heart starting to race for no apparent reason: this is known as *clear feeling*. Or it might prefer to be a voice inside your head or even a whisper in your ear in the form of a word, sound, or song: this power of sound is known as *clear hearing*. This voice is your higher self dropping down some wisdom or knocking you on the side of the head and saying, "Listen up!" Your intuition may also choose a more visual form of communication and paint a picture or play a mini movie in your mind's eye: this intuitive form is known as *clear seeing*. Perhaps your intuition will also use the sense of smell to get your attention. Suddenly you may smell a fragrance or odor that connects you back to a person, a place, or a loved one: this is known as *clear smelling*. Lastly you might get a flash of insight, a feeling that you just know

in your bones something to be true and you do not know how you know it: this is called *clear knowing*. Most of us have one or two main ways in which our intuition talks. Sometimes these messages are clear and direct, but more often than not they come in more subtle forms of symbols, hunches, whispers, and feelings. It is up to us to get present, listen, and pay attention.

3. Play Games

The more we can approach our intuition from a place of wonder and delight, the more easily it will flow. Try creating simple games to engage. For example, when the phone rings, before you check the screen, guess to see who it might be. Going to meet a friend, imagine what color they might be wearing. Tune into a friend before reaching out and guess how they are feeling. Come up with your own way to play. Keep it light, playful, and fun.

4. Divination Tools

Tarot cards, spiritual books, runes, a pendulum, whatever strikes your fancy. Every morning I start my day with the question: *What do I need to know today to have my best, most aligned day possible?* I then do a simple 1- to 3-card Tarot reading to receive the answer. You can use any of your favorite tools to do this, even open a book to a "random" page to see what guidance it holds—this is called *bibliomancy*. Other questions I ask are:

What is helpful for me to know today? What should I be aware of today? What should I focus on? What is for my highest good and harm to none? You can, of course, curate your own questions to ask yourself.

5. The Dream World

Try keeping a dream journal. This is especially useful for those of you who do not think you dream or have a hard time remembering your dreams. It is super easy and only takes 3 to 5 minutes. Keep a journal by your bedside, and as soon as you wake up in the morning, even before you go to the bathroom (if you can), write down anything and everything you remember. The people that were there, where you were, what you were doing, the emotions that you felt. Include every detail from the wild and wacky to the most mundane. The practice of writing your dreams down builds a bridge between your mind's conscious and unconscious realms—a result of this connection is an increased flow of inner guidance.

So you can better see an example of how these techniques can work, here is a story from a student of mine named Sammy. Sammy was in a new and seemingly fantastic relationship, but there was a problem—she had this strange feeling she could not shake. She didn't know if it was her own fear of being in a relationship or if her intuition was trying to tell her something, so she decided to turn to the dreamworld for help to decipher the answer. About two weeks after she started the practice, Sammy's message arrived. Her heart pounded hard as she woke up in the middle of the night from the most vivid dream she had experienced in some time. In the dream, she and her partner had just had sex. She had gotten up to go to the bathroom and get them both some water, and when she returned, he was texting someone with a sly look on his face. Her heart immediately sank, and the uneasy feeling she had been fighting for weeks returned. Sammy asked if she could see his phone, but he was so captivated by his text he didn't even hear her. So she asked again. He began taunting her by saying, "You want to see this phone?" and began pulling out other phones repeating, "Or do you want to see this phone?" This game went on for some time until he threw all the phones into the air. He looked her in the eye and simply said, "I am sorry."

Sammy awoke before the phones hit the ground. But, still enraptured by the positive state of their relationship in the waking world, she chalked the dream up to a nightmare and dismissed the guidance. To her disbelief, two days later almost the exact same scenario played out, only this time there was no waking from the nightmare. In the "real life version" there was only one phone, and he did toss it to her. Without explanation, he got dressed, took his phone back, and said

those same words—"I am sorry"—as he walked out the door.

Like Sammy, many of us do not trust or listen to our guidance when we receive it. I believe Sammy knew her answer all along, and this was why she couldn't shake that icky feeling. It's easy to get caught in denial and ignore what is going on right in front of your face. But each time you show up, dial in, and listen closely, you will deepen your relationship to your inner guidance and excavate your buried treasure a little bit more. Be brave, trust your intuition, and take action as you unwrap this gift of your Ajna Chakra.

A GODDESS/GOD LIKE NO OTHER

As you know by now, shakti is the wild, dynamic, and creative expression of power and bliss. Shiva is pure consciousness and awareness, the ground of being, from which shakti springs forth. In tantra there is a saying: *Shakti without shiva is total mayhem, but shiva without shakti is but a corpse.* It is through the union of their opposite yet complementary forces that we find an integrated wholeness or oneness with self. Within this place of oneness, we come into deeper levels of understanding and knowing, and our authentic creative power and magic are birthed. At the mystical Ajna center, the pingala nadi (the solar channel) and ida nadi

(the lunar channel) dissolve into one. This intersection marks the shift from the dual to the non-dual consciousness, from seeing with our two eyes to seeing with the clarity of the merged third eye.

Ardhanarishvara, the presiding deity of the Sixth Chakra, is the ultimate symbol of this powerful weaving into wholeness and oneness.

Ardhanarishvara defies the typical binaries within which we typically operate. They are the all-gender inclusive—half goddess and half god, half female and half male, the embodiment of both Shakti and Shiva. They are the "totality that lies beyond duality." Ardhanarishvara is typically depicted with four arms: two belonging to Shakti and two belonging to Shiva.

Shakti makes up the left half of Ardhanarishvara's body and holds the energy of the moon, which represents the feeling qualities of intuition, creativity, spontaneity, and deep soul nourishment. It is also the side of the body containing the heart and speaks to her unconditional love. She holds a lotus flower in one of her hands and a staff in the other. Both are symbols of purity, beauty, and knowledge. She wears a beautiful sari and is adorned in gold jewelry.

Shiva makes up the right half of Ardhanarishvara, which holds the energy of the sun, of action, logic, valor, and linear thought. He holds a trident in one hand and the mudra of fearlessness, abhaya, in the other, which we saw Kali and Lakshmi also hold. The three-pronged trident is a symbol that holds many meanings, from unity in mind/body/spirit to past/present/future to ida/pingala/sushumna. Shiva's hair is matted with dreadlocks and writhing with snakes, and he wears animal skin. The two halves share a single third eye, the emblem for the awakened eye that no longer sees through the eyes of judgment, limitation, or separateness but instead sees through the eyes of beauty, love, truth, and curiosity.

Ardhanarishvara teaches us there is no separation between these necessary halves of our whole. Shakti is inseparable from Shiva, and Shiva is inseparable from Shakti. They are dancing together in every single cell of our being. When we develop this unity within ourselves, we ultimately find freedom.

A simple prayer or mantra I use to connect with Ardhanarishvara and to receive their empowerments is, *I honor the whole of me.* You can try saying it now. "I honor the whole of me." Pause for a moment. Take a deep breath in and release a deep breath out. Close your two eyes to allow the third to see and repeat it again, slowly: "I honor the whole of me." Tune

in and feel what arises. I find that one of two things can happen when working with this prayer: First, your consciousness may direct you to the places within yourself that you have cast out, rejected, or denied, and therefore are not honoring. This awareness acts as a guiding light to return you to wholeness. The second thing you may experience is a filling and expanding sensation that stems from the divine light of grace, peace, and unconditional love. This celestial positivity highlights your inherent worth. Allow yourself to rest in this spacious energy as it flows into every nook and cranny of your being. When you honor this wholeness of *you*, magic ensues!

The real magic happens when we move beyond the binary and do not rely on logic alone, but instead blend our intuitive and objective realities and see through both the two eyes and the third. What results is a more integrated self with access to deeper levels of truth, peace, beauty, and aliveness. The following practices are here to help you ignite the light of your soul and illuminate the power of your Ajna Chakra.

THE PRACTICES: 7 DAYS OF MAGIC

Day One: Altar

Your Third-Eye Altar is the place you will come to every day for your Ajna Chakra rituals. Fill it with items that ignite magic, invoke beauty, and awaken a sense of playfulness. Don't be afraid to put on your chakra-colored glasses and stretch your imagination when creating your sacred space. Have fun and remember your illuminated power comes when you honor the whole of you!

Let's start with the essentials:

Altar Essentials

- Something purple (cloth, candle, crystal, paper, paint)
- Candle, lamp, or something to represent *light*
- An item that represents the magical realms (magic wand, crystal ball, tarot cards, lucky charm, etc.)

Altar Inspirations

At the Ajna doorway, it is nice to feel the support of the five elements: Earth, Water, Fire, Air, and Space. You might consider having something that represents each of the elements to you. Below is a list of possible examples—do not let them limit you!

Earth: plants, flowers, soil, stones

Water: a chalice of water, rose water, essential oils, moon blood

Fire: candle

Air: Something to burn (white sage, palo santo, piñon, incense), a feather

Space: singing bowls, chimes, rattle, a bell, playing any music that inspires you

Light: mirror (to see your divine reflection)

Additional suggestions

Dream catcher

Dream journal

Book of spiritual wisdom you are studying or would like to

Vision board

Crystals: labradorite, lapis lazuli, azurite

Essential oils: magnolia, copaiba, clary sage

Tarot cards: The Magician, The High Priestess, Six of Fire, Eight of Fire

Refer to the Quick Charts in the Appendix for extended meanings of crystals, oils, and tarot cards.

Writing Contemplation

1. List 10 things you enjoy just for fun and play. When was the last time you allowed yourself to do any of these? Pick one to do this week.

2. When you imagine something, you create an act of magic. What is your belief around magic? Can you make a list of at least 5 things that have happened in your life that could be considered an act of magic?

3. Do you have fear around what you might see if you opened your third eye? If yes, why?

Day Two: Mudra—Jnana Mudra

The mudra for the Ajna Chakra is one of my favorites. It is a variation of one of the most well-known mudras, called jnana mudra. *Jnana* means "knowledge," or "embodied wisdom." In the classical version, the tip of the thumb and the tip of the index finger come together while the other three fingers softly extend and rest on the thighs with the palms down. Your index finger represents the individual soul, human consciousness; the small self, and your thumb represents the universal soul, cosmic consciousness; the divine or higher self. Through creating this seal, the human you merges with the divine you. The version we are going to practice holds this beautiful teaching and shape but adds another level of intricacy as it recruits the other six fingers to intertwine and wrap around one another, symbolic of how the pingala and ida nadis intertwine above and below each chakra, creating a powerful vortex of energy which makes the chakras spin. It also speaks to the union of all of who we are, and specifically the shiva (masculine) and shakti (feminine) energies, and the ruling deity of the Sixth Chakra, Ardhanarishvara.

At first it might seem like gymnastics for your hands and fingers, so do the best you can and know your hands and fingers will get more supple, just like your body when you do your yoga practice.

Here are the step-by-step instructions.

1. Find a comfortable seat in front of your altar. Sit up tall, ground your pelvis, and drop a grounding cord.

2. Supercharge your hands (see page 22 if you need a refresher).

3. Inhale, reach your arms up overhead, and cross your right wrist over your left. Keeping the wrists crossed, lower the shape down to the level of the Anahata Chakra at the heart.

4. Bring the backs of your hands together.

5. Wrap your right pinky finger around the left.

6. Wrap your right ring finger around the left.

7. Wrap your right middle finger around the left.

8. Connect the tips of your index fingers to the tips of your thumbs completing the seal of jnana mudra.

9. Soften your eyes or close them and stay here for at least 10 deep *nourishing breaths*.

10. When you are ready go ahead and release the mudra. If you would like to try on the second side crossing left wrist over right you are welcome to. Just know this may take a little practice!

You can also listen to the how-to audio at www.chakrarituals.com.

Writing contemplation

1. What does honoring the whole of you mean to you and your life?

2. Is there one side of you that tends to dominate and take over? How can Ardhanarishvara help you to restore balance?

3. Where are you caught in denial or illusion? Is there something that is going on in your life that you are not seeing?

Day Three: Breath—Nadi Shodhana

This pranayama practice will bring you clarity of vision and peace of mind. Unlike the heating breaths you've experienced in the Third and Fifth Chakra rituals—kapalabhati and simhasana—Nadi Shodhana is a cooling breath designed to soothe and rejuvenate the nervous system. It purifies the subtle energy channels or rivers of light in the body. Recall that *nadi* means "energy channel" and *shodhana* means "purification." Also commonly known as "alternate nostril breathing," or "sun and moon breath" because it helps to restore balance between the solar and lunar energies in the body, the sympathetic and parasympathetic nervous systems, and the energy of action and receptivity.

My favorite times to practice nadi shodhana are at the end of my yoga practice right before savasana, before meditation, or at the sunset or twilight hours. The technique serves as a healing balm to calm and clear the mind. Practice it anytime you crave balance, deep restoration, and want to arouse your cosmic vision.

Let's get started.

1. Find a comfortable, grounded seat. Hands rest on your knees or thighs.

2. Take three deep breaths, inhaling and exhaling out through both nostrils.

3. With your right hand make a peace sign and lightly place your peace fingers to your third eye center, the Ajna doorway.

4. Place the tip of your ring finger lightly to your left nostril and the tip of your thumb lightly to your right nostril.

5. Inhale through both nostrils, pause, gently close off the right nostril and exhale through the left nostril for the count of 3.

6. Pause. Inhale through the left nostril for the count of 3. Pause.

7. Gently close off the left nostril and exhale through the right nostril for the count of 3. Pause.

8. Inhale through the right nostril for the count of 3.

9. Close off the right nostril and exhale through the left nostril for the count of 3.

Continue in this rhythm for 2 to 3 minutes focusing your awareness on the pathway of breath. Switch nostrils on each exhale.

You can also listen to the how-to audio at www.chakrarituals.com.

Other Benefits:

Releases stress and anxiety

Balances the right and left hemispheres of the brain

Combats fatigue

Writing Contemplation

1. What are the ways in which your intuition likes to get your attention? How do you receive your messages from your inner guidance?

2. Think of a recent time when you trusted and followed your intuition. What was the result?

3. Think of another time where you dismissed or ignored your intuition for whatever reason. What was the impact of that?

As I mentioned at the start of the chapter, once we have reached the Ajna doorway in our chakra journey, we have mostly moved out of the body and into the worlds of spirit and the mind. This body prayer will be a way for you to symbolically connect to your Sixth Chakra through physical touch and body postures.

Since this is your vision center, you *may* choose to play with doing this sequence with your eyes closed. If closing your eyes seems too daunting, try taking really long blinks. Notice how your lens of perspective changes dramatically when we rely only on our inner sight. For safety, please only try this after the sequence is memorized and fully embodied as part of your practice.

Suggested use: Repeat the sequence 1 to 3 times on each side. Follow the pictures to come or watch the how-to video at www.chakrarituals.com.

Start standing, feet hip-width apart, hands in prayer, thumbs lightly touching the Ajna center.

1. Inhale; open elbows wide and lift chest. Exhale; return hands to prayer, thumbs to third eye. Repeat 3 times

2. Wrap your right arm underneath the left for eagle arms. Bend your knees, sit down into chair pose. Hinge at your hips and bring your chest to your thighs

3. Release your hands down. Inhale; elongate the spine and sweep your left leg up and back

4. Exhale; round the spine, bring your knee in towards your third eye center

5. Step your left leg back, low lunge

6. Inhale; rise to high lunge with eagle arms (right arm wraps underneath the left)

7. Hands to prayer, thumbs lightly touching the Ajna center

8. Inhale, open elbows wide and lift chest; Exhale, pulse elbows back together. Repeat steps 7–8 three more times

9. Hands down, step back to high plank pose; inhale

10. Exhale; lower to the belly, extend arms, third eye to the earth

11. Push back to downward-facing dog

13. Step to the top of the mat, roll up to standing, hands to prayer at your third eye

Repeat on the second side, wrapping the left arm underneath the right and stepping the right leg back.

Writing Contemplation

1. What is the lens of perception through which you view the world? Do you see through the "default" eyes or through the "real" eyes?

2. What colors your perception?

3. Many of us have to train our eyes to see the beauty within ourselves and the world. What is beauty to you? Make a list of 5 beautiful things you have seen today.

Day Five: Meditation—Inner Wise Woman Who Knows

No one knows you better than you. No one knows what you need more than you. Within all of us is an inner wise woman who knows greater depths and truths, who knows how to heal, how to laugh, how to love, how to be vulnerable and powerful, and doesn't give a flying "f*ck" what anyone else thinks. This guided visualization is going to take you on a journey into yourself to meet and receive the blessings that only you can give. Instead of looking outside yourself for the answers, let's turn our attention inward and meet our Inner Wise Woman.

1. Come into a comfortable seated position.

2. Rub your hands together vigorously until they are nice and hot. Place your cupped palms over your eyes, bathing your eyes in the heat and in the darkness. Take a deep breath in and a deep breath out.

3. Release your hands but keep your eyes gently closed, bringing your inner gaze to your third eye center.

4. Imagine this center opening and the most magnificent light shining out and onto a screen directly in front of you. This is the space known as *chidakash*, the space where the unconscious, the conscious, and the super-conscious minds come together. It is here that the mind of your dreams, intuition, and imagination gets to play with your *cosmic vision*.

5. Think about your most favorite place on planet Earth. Is it a beautiful beach, the forest, a mountaintop, a country? Or maybe it is your home? Whatever it is, see it coming into focus on the screen before you and take three deep *nourishing breaths*.

6. Off in the distance, you see a beautiful older woman moving towards you. How does she approach? Maybe she is walking, dancing, riding a bike or a surfboard; or is she driving in a car? Anything is possible. As she gets closer, notice what she is wearing, how her hair is styled, even the

jewelry or makeup she may or may not have on. Take in everything that you see. Invite all your senses to play (the sounds, the smells, the taste, and even touch) as you allow this picture to come into focus.

7. You're now standing face-to-face with this woman. As you look into her eyes, you realize these are your eyes. As you look at her smile, you laugh inside, as this is your smile. She opens her arms and wraps them around you, giving you the most beautiful embrace. She whispers in your ear and says, "I have been expecting you."

8. This is your time to ask your wiser older self anything you want to know, anything that will support your growth and healing, anything that you need some gentle guidance on. No topic or question is off limits. Just drop into your heart. Ask and listen for the answers.

9. When you feel like you're complete, that you've asked everything you've wanted to ask, thank her for showing up today and ask her if there is a name she would like you to call her. *Listen for her name.*

10. Before you say goodbye for now, your Inner Wise Woman offers you a gift. This gift may be in the form of a symbol, a color, a word, or an object.

11. As you thank her again, she reminds you to come back and visit any time. She reminds you to go inside, and within, you will find a guide that is willing and able to

illuminate your path every step of the way.

12. Bring your attention back to your body. Take a deep, full, rich breath in. Open your mouth and let it go. And another deep breath in and deep full breath out.

13. Bring your hands into a prayer at your heart, then to your third eye and bow to the Inner Wise One Who Knows. Namaste.

14. As soon as you finish, take out your journal and begin the writing contemplation practices below.

You can also listen to the how-to audio at www.chakrarituals.com.

Writing Contemplation

1. Take a few moments to write about your experience. What did your Inner Wise Women look like? Did she have a name? What messages did she offer you? Write, draw, or paint everything that you saw and that you remember.

2. The first time I did an exercise like this, I was given a beautiful vintage hand mirror. I was told this was no ordinary mirror, but a mirror that only allows one to see through the eyes of truth and love. My inner wise woman called it my *goddess mirror* and said it was time to see beyond the illusion and to see what others truly saw in me. Needless to say, I cried. What was the gift that your inner wise woman offered you? Remember, it could be in the

form of an object, symbol, color, or word. Write down whatever you recall. And do not worry if today you didn't see or hear anything. We are working to develop sensitivity, to open our vision center to see inside, beyond reason, and come into contact with wisdom that lives inside of you. If you have never done anything like this before, it may take some time to awaken this sensitivity.

3. What dreams have you set aside and/or have you forgotten about? Maybe you had a dream of writing a children's book, recording an album, or dancing on stage with Beyoncé. Maybe you dreamed of traveling the world, speaking a foreign language, living in a community, having a garden and growing your own food, or maybe you dreamed of starting your own business, going to Burning Man, or of becoming a mother. Make a list of all the dreams you have set aside. What led you to stop pursuing your dream(s)? What dreams are you ready to start pursuing today?

Day Six: Embodiment—Vision Board

I have experienced the power of visualization ever since I was a young girl training for the Olympics in the sport of platform diving. Visualization techniques were part of our daily practice. My coach would have us climb up the ladder to the ten-meter platform and stand at the edge of the tower and visualize our dive. He would even go as far as giving us feedback on our visualized dive and would prep us for the next dive to come. This type of training led my teammate and good friend Laura Wilkinson to the gold medal podium at the 2000 Olympics. She had broken her foot just months before the Olympic Games and was severely limited in her ability to physically train. For most athletes, that would've been the end of their Olympic pursuit, but not for Laura. She doubled down on her mental training and became the first American woman in our lifetime to bring home Olympic gold in this event!

After all this practice with visualization techniques and witnessing their power, when I first heard of creating a vision board as a way to help guide me in the direction of my dreams, it didn't seem to be in the least bit woo-woo to me. If anything, it helped ground my vision into a tangible, beautiful form and became a blueprint for that period of my life. I love the practice of creating a vision board for the Sixth Chakra, as it is the place in which we dream and imagine from, where we get our flashes of insights, and where the magical process of manifestation begins. By taking our insights, images, words, colors, and symbols and creatively turning them into a work of art, we begin to actively engage with downward-flowing currents of manifestation and embodiment. A big first step in grounding our vision into a reality. When we look at our vision daily, we strengthen and align it within our psyche, soul, and heart.

So let's start envisioning and creating.

Suggested supplies

Poster board or cork board of any size

Scissors

Glue stick, tape, pins

Lots and lots of magazines

Glitter, paint, markers

Stickers

Pictures

Any other fun, creative stuff you may want to include

Before you begin

Take a moment to ground yourself and close your eyes.

Take a deep *nourishing breath*.

Imagine it is one year from now. One year from now, what are you doing? Where are you living? Who are you with? What do you see?

Take your time, and in your mind's eye paint in all the details that you can. Invite your senses in to play. What do you taste, smell, hear, and touch?

What is your feeling state? Happy, sad, excited, nervous, peaceful?

Begin to collect images, words, colors, and symbols that will inspire you and support your growth and transformation on this journey of bringing your vision to life. You can include things like your dream job, the new home you will be living in, the book you just wrote, you standing on the top of the podium at the Olympic Games, or you with the partner of your dreams. Once you have all your images, you will arrange them on your board and glue them down.

Remember, pictures have the ability to evoke feelings, memories, and beauty; they give us hope; and most importantly inspire us to *take action*!

A few additional tips

Have fun and be creative!

As my teacher Brenda Rose says, "Stop trying to get it right because you can't get it wrong!"

Be sure to use words, colors, pictures, and symbols that are uplifting and make you feel good.

Consider including an actual picture of you.

If you feel overwhelmed, you can opt to focus on just one area of your life such as personal or professional life.

Have a vision board party with a few of your sisters.

Take a picture of your vision board with your phone so you can continually be inspired wherever you may go.

Writing Contemplation

1. Creating your vision board is not enough for magic to ensue. A vision without action remains a dream. As you see your vision, your dream, before you, what action will you take this month, this week, today, this moment to start to move you in the direction of manifesting this dream into reality?

2. Whether you have stepped foot onto the Playa at Burning Man or not, I want you to put on your magical chakra-colored glasses and reimagine what is possible at this time on planet Earth.

3. What does fulfilling your greatest potential look and feel like?

Day Seven: Lessons from Your Mystical Eye of Empowerment

- Your world awakens when you open and see through all three eyes!

- Explore with childlike wonderment; make time to play, daydream, and frolic in the realms of the unimaginable.

- Intuition is Magic in Action. The best way to align with it is through a daily meditation practice.

- Your intuition speaks to you in five ways: through clear feeling, seeing, hearing, smelling, or knowing. Get to know your preferred style of communication.

- Within you is an Inner Wise Woman who knows; allow her to be your mentor, your guide.

- Dreams come from a divine source; as we move towards our dreams, we move towards the divine.[2]

- A vision is just the first step on the path of manifestation; to ground your dreams into reality you MUST take action!

You've stretched your imagination, played with your intuition, crafted a vision, and opened your three eyes to see the beauty and truth of the Real World. You have merged into oneness and moved beyond the illusion of separateness and into the stunning purity of light. You are now ready to take the final step on your chakra journey. You are now ready to take the seat of the throne and be crowned the queen of your queendom.

Today is your day of reflection and rest. Take some time to reflect upon your most important takeaway from this chakra chapter. If there was only one thing you could remember from this chapter, what would it be? Maybe take a moment to note it down as we continue the journey, that one thing that you want to remember. Now is also the perfect opportunity to return to any of the previous days' exercises or readings.

This whole universe is a path of liberation,
A vast arena for your endless play.
Playing, let your awareness be everywhere at once.
Planets, stars, swirling galaxies, subatomic motes—
All are dancing within you.
Enter the rhythm,
Descend into the space between the beats.
Dissolve into intimacy with the Dancing One.

—The Radiance Sutras: Sutra 33

9

The Crown Jewel

THE SEVENTH CHAKRA

We have made it to the final stop on our color-filled journey through the chakras. With each chakra you have investigated, you have gained new empowerments, insights, and understandings. You have excavated and polished each of the precious gems of intelligence and become more embodied, intimately aware, and alive. Now it is time to take the seat of the throne and activate the crown jewel, known as Sahasrara.

The Seventh Chakra, or Crown Chakra, is represented by a beautiful lotus flower that lives on the top of the head, connecting you to the infinite. It is here that our deepest longing resides. The longing to feel at home in the universe and the longing to be in communion with God. This is the god of your own unique understanding, whether it be the Goddess, Jesus, Buddha, the Universe, Higher Consciousness, or Self. Just as a lotus flower unfurls its petals to soak in nutrients from the sun, the Crown Chakra opens us up to the heavens, drinks in the amrita (divine nectar) of grace, and awakens our spiritual power. The roots of the lotus reach all the way down to the earth, infusing this limitless divine intelligence into every cell of our being.

Sahasrara wakes us up from our complacency and helps us remember our own divinity. To see the miracles in the mundane, to celebrate this gift of life, and to experience the divine thread of connection that runs through all living things. The crown creates union with heaven and earth, enlightenment and embodiment, and is the power that merges the small self with the higher self, the individual soul with the cosmic soul.

With the crown jewel now in place and your full power ignited, you are ready to be crowned.

ANATOMY OF THE CROWN CHAKRA

The Sahasrara Chakra includes the crown of the head and the space right above it. It is the place in which the soul enters the body. You can imagine it as an aperture that connects you to a realm that is boundless, outside of structure and form, and is even beyond language. Therefore, the yantra, the visual depiction of the chakra, becomes a much more meaningful and helpful tool here. The crown yantra is an emblem of exquisite beauty that has been referred to by many different names—the nirvana (transcendent) yantra, the soma (the nectar of the gods) yantra, and the thousand heads of white light—each a metaphor for the path

of enlightenment. As we take a closer look at each of the shapes and symbols encapsulated in the yantra, we gain a more poetic understanding of the essence and intelligence of the crown jewel.

At the center of the yantra there is a circle. The circle represents the fullness and the luminescence of moonlight. The moon is the light within the darkness and represents the depths of our being: the shadows, the mysterious, the sacred feminine, and the dream world. Surrounding the full moon is a lotus flower with 1,008 petals, a number in yoga philosophy for the infinite, inspiring us to blossom into higher levels of consciousness. The lotus flower is a symbol for the macrocosm and the microcosm, and it represents the divinity of the cosmos and the divinity of (wo)mankind. Emanating out in all directions from behind the lotus flower is a golden shimmering halo created by the radiance of the sun.

The Crown Chakra is beyond an element, a sense, or even a bija sound. It is traditionally depicted as bright white light—white being the color that contains all other hues of the rainbow—or as violet with a gold aura.

YOUR CHAKRA CHEAT SHEET

Name	Sahasrara
Meaning	Lotus of a thousand petals
Physical Location	Top of the head or slightly above the crown
Element	Beyond an Element
Color	White, Violet, Gold or all the colors of the rainbow
Sense	Beyond

Bija Sound	Beyond a Bija Sound
Vowel Sound	EEEEE
Energetics	Cosmic Consciousness Transcendence Seat of Spirituality
Affirmations	I know. I am one with all of existence. Divinity resides in me. Universal wisdom is always available to me. I belong to the source of all things. I am free! Thank YOU.

Body parts related	Crown of the head, Skull, Cranial bones, Cranial nerves, Nervous system
Effects of Deficiency	Spiritual Cynicism Fear of spirituality and/or religion Over-identification with the material world Disconnected from Self and Spirit Feeling of separation from others
Effect of Excess	Overly intellectual—living "in the head" Dissociation from the body Spiritual Elitism (my yoga is better than your yoga) Fanatical religious or spiritual ideas Spiritual Bypass
Balance	Spiritual Intelligence Experience of inner peace and gratitude Able to see life as a gift Connected to a Higher Power Feels interconnected to all living things Sees the Divine in all things Embodied Wisdom

Imagine the most beautiful crown placed on the top of your head. It is bright gold with seven brilliant gems shining in all the hues of the rainbow: red, orange, yellow, green, blue, purple, and white. This is no ordinary crown; it acts as a satellite dish attuning you to the divine. It is here you gain the understanding that the divine consciousness running the universe, which allows the sun to rise, the moon to set, and the stars to shine, is the same energy that is coursing through you. As a queen, it is your duty to bring the intelligence of the heavens down to earth and integrate both the spiritual and physical worlds. Here are four ways to help you do this:

1. **Discerning Spiritual Bypass**

   At the beginning of my yoga journey, I fell in love with one of my teachers, something that may not be looked upon favorably but happens all the time. He was super spiritual; performed all kinds of wild rituals I had never seen before; and had Indian gurus, and even an astrologer, on speed dial. I was completely fascinated and enamored by this whole new world he was opening me up to. Everything was "love and light" . . . even when it wasn't. And if I questioned something that didn't quite fit into the category of what I perceived to be love and light, I was told that *if I was spiritually evolved enough I would understand.* Being new on my path and a naive seeker, I believed it to be true.

I have now been on my yogic path for over twenty years, and I can say that hands-down the biggest downfall in these communities is the overemphasis on the "love and the light." I know right now you might be a little confused and thinking something like, *Wait, I thought the path to enlightenment was seeing through the eyes of love and being guided by the divine light—right?* And yes, that is true, but NOT when the use of false or superficial "love and light" becomes an escape mechanism to avoid taking responsibility for one's actions; not showing up, doing your own deeper work, or looking at your own shadow. Your shadow is the parts of yourself that you keep hidden in the dark. This may be your deepest fears, your vulnerability, your anger, your unresolved, unfaced trauma, or core conditioning; it may also be your greatness.

Back in the 1980s, Buddhist teacher and psychotherapist John Welwood coined the term *spiritual bypass* to address this self-avoidance process. He defined spiritual bypassing as "a way of using spiritual ideas and practices to sidestep or avoid painful feelings, taking responsibility, or facing unresolved emotional issues or psychological wounds."[1] When we turn our backs on our shadow and our own pain, we may appear "at one" with the universe to others while actually becoming further fragmented, numb, and detached.

Robert Augustus Masters refers to spiritual bypassing as a kind of analgesic drug—helping us check out rather than check in.[2] The goal of the Crown Chakra and the chakra system overall is to come into full embodiment, wholeness, integration, and freedom—none of which are possible if we are hiding behind the guise of "if you were spiritual enough, you would understand." Spiritual dissociation is still dissociation. Recall the beloved flower of the chakra system, the lotus. The lotus is a symbol of our journey to embodiment and enlightenment. It grows in the mud and has its roots deep in the earth. The mud represents our shadow, our wounds; the conscious and the unconscious places within us that need to be tended to, nourished, and healed. From there the lotus rises up in the direction of the light and blossoms open—there is no bypass or workaround through the mud—it grows right through it. We must do the same. The reward that comes with your crown is radical aliveness, "integrity, depth, and love; a life of authenticity, where all is honored, a life lived to its fullest."[3]

2. Gratitude as Divine Principle

If the only prayer you ever say in your entire life is thank you, it will be enough.

—Meister Eckhart

According to Robert Emmons, the world's leading researcher on gratitude, gratitude is "a felt sense of wonder, thankfulness, and appreciation for life."[4] The Indian guru Swami Rama adds that gratitude means "falling in love with life." Both these perspectives and more belong to the Sahasrara Chakra, which shows that gratitude moves us out of complacency and entitlement and awakens us to the gifts of life. It attunes us to our hearts and allows us to see the miracles within the perceived ordinariness of everyday existence.

You can think of gratitude as the soma: the nectar of the divine, the elixir of bliss. When we express gratitude and appreciation for our life, we transform. The infinite petals of the lotus flower unfold and soak in this divine sweetness—it seeps down through the crown of the head and nourishes as it fills every chakra and therefore the whole of our being. To me the soma of gratitude is a divine investiture, the knowingness that when I am grateful, I am connected with and being filled with God. This is why I call gratitude a divine principle.

Science has proven that gratitude changes us on the physical, psychological, and social levels. It strengthens our immune system and lowers our blood pressure, increases tendency toward positive emotions, helps us be more compassionate and outgoing; it improves our relationships, helps us live longer, and increases our overall sense of satisfaction—all of which makes us not only healthier but happier.[5] Gratitude asks us to focus on and bring our attention to the good in our life, onto what is working, and to see the blessings that we have received, both small and large. You can think of gratitude as an affirmation, a mini celebration, with each honoring. The more you do this, the more positivity and good you will attract and the more your life will appreciate.

Now, I am not suggesting you ignore the challenges, hardships, and difficulties in your life—that would just be another form of spiritual bypassing. What I am suggesting is that you bring equal emphasis to the good in your life—especially in the darker times—and recognize them as seeds of divine hope.

It is so easy to take life for granted, to miss the magic in a moment, and to fall prey to a negative mindset and way of being. When this happens, the petals of the Crown Chakra collapse down and close onto themselves, limiting our access to divine grace. That is why the practice of gratitude is so incredibly powerful and helpful. The good news is the crown aperture can open as easily as it closes in as little as sixty seconds, actually. Let's give it a try. When you find a natural moment in this paragraph, close your eyes for a moment. Tune into your senses, listen to the tidal rhythm of your breath, feel the movements of your chest as it flows in and out, and let your mind drop into your heart. Then think of one thing you are grateful for right now. Maybe it is your lover's smile, the view outside your window, the chocolate croissant you had for breakfast, the stranger who held the door for you, the perfect parking spot you scored, or the ways you are showing up for yourself today. As you allow yourself to delve into the full feeling of this gift, you align with a force greater than yourself and open to the heavens.

When we adhere to this principle, we can more easily remember what an incredible miracle it is to be alive. That life is a cause for celebration, that the fact that you woke up this morning, and have air in your lungs to breathe, is enough to celebrate and to be grateful for. No matter what challenges you face, what obstacles are on your path, life is still coursing through your veins, which means divine grace does as well.

3. BE your own Guru

For many years, instead of going to therapy, I opted for healers, energy workers, psychics, astrologers, and gurus. Now, technically, there is nothing wrong with this, except when you begin to trust and empower their opinions over your own. For a period of several years, there was one incredible healer/energy worker that I had regular healing sessions with.

I found them so profound I would gift sessions with her to many of my closest friends so they too could experience this same deep healing and wisdom. Days before my fortieth birthday, I decided to gift myself a session as a way to start off a new decade and a pinnacle birthday. It felt important.

As the session began, she asked me who the new man was in my life. I looked at her funny and said there was no man. She replied, "Yes, there is. I sense a man who is very much in your space." She went on to describe him in detail, "six feet tall, mixed-race, dark eyes, and long, wavy hair." Of course, I liked what I was hearing, but still, told her, "nope," because I definitely hadn't met the guy she spoke of. She then told me, "Well, get ready because he's coming, and when you meet him, he is going to be *the one*." In all the years I had been working with this woman, she had never given me this kind of detailed information about someone, so I was intrigued.

A few days later, I was teaching a yoga class at a local Venice spot, and next thing you know, the man she described walked into the room! I did my best to keep my composure and just teach the class. After the class finished, I stayed behind to talk to a few students, and I assumed he had left, but when I walked out of the door, there he was—waiting for me. He introduced himself, thanked me

for class, and then asked if he could take me out for lunch. Without hesitation, I said, "Yes!" (which is completely out of character for me). But as soon as I got to lunch, I realized something was off— something just wasn't right. Everything about it, from our conversation to his advances; our connection felt misguided, misaligned, and weird. But because of the premonition from my healer, I overlooked all of this. I convinced myself that he must be perfect, and I was the problem, and that I was scared and closed off to love, so I allowed him to take me on another date. A few days later, he and I were walking down the street and literally ran into my healer—the same one that had the premonition. She hugged me and whispered in my ear, "This is the guy!" That was all the validation I needed to completely override my instincts about him. A few weeks later, the truth came out. And this guy was not at all my Prince Charming, but more of a womanizing stalker and inconsiderate dirt bag. My body and spirit warned me of this truth from the start, but I overrode its messages because I trusted the words and insights of my healer more than my own. I considered her more spiritual, powerful, tapped-in, and connected than I did myself! The thing is, my healer was right—he was in my "energetic space" for some time, because for weeks before we met, he had been stalking me online to plan the "picture-perfect" run-in! And it worked. If I had only listened and trusted my own inner wisdom—my crown jewel—my own guidance, and my connection to spirit, I would have saved myself a lot of pain and suffering.

The lesson here is for you to be your own guru, your own guide. This is not to say that teachers or healers can't help you on your journey, but they never know the next steps of our journey better than we do. Trust yourself. This is why it's so important to hone your connection to your Crown Chakra—so that when your intuition throws red flags and sounds the alarm, even in spite of someone else's advice, you'll be able to listen. You are in the pilot's seat. No more BLINDLY giving your power and trust to someone else over your own instincts, no matter how smart, wise, or spiritually evolved they may be.

4. Here to Serve

You are the conduit through which the divine flows, moving from heaven above to earth below. From my own experience, I can testify that the yoga practice can strengthen your vessel to hold all this energy, so that you can become a vessel of love—here to serve.

Taking the seat of the teacher was one of the most confronting and best things I've ever done. It is something I resisted for a very long time, so I spent the first of my many years in the yoga world on the business side—managing other teachers' careers, running studios and a retreat business.

Then one day one of my teachers came into my office, got in my face, and said, "You are hiding behind this desk. What are you so afraid of?!" His words struck me at the core, and in that moment, I realized I *was* hiding. It was safe for me to be behind the desk. I knew how to do that, I was good at it, and it made sense. Teaching yoga, on the other hand, felt anything but safe. The practice of yoga cracked me open and connected me to my body, heart, spirit, and femininity, which left me feeling vulnerable and exposed. Although I knew this practice was completely transforming my life, I thought, "Who am I to be sharing it?" Especially living in Venice, California, and sitting at the helm of one of the most influential yoga studios in the world, managing many of the teachers that shaped yoga in the West.

But one day everything changed. A teacher who I managed did not show up for class, leaving fifty students just waiting alone in the yoga room. At that moment, I had two choices: send everyone home with a comp pass to come back or step out from behind the desk and teach the class myself. I remember just sitting there at my desk, looking at myself in the mirror, locked in fear, and seriously contemplating sending everyone

home, when the voice inside my head shifted. *If this practice is really about serving and helping people, who am I not to be sharing it?* Then I stood up, put my big-girl yoga pants on, said a prayer to get out of my own way, and walked into the room to serve. And on that day, my life changed forever.

There are so many ways to serve and to be a vessel for the benefit of others. And often the opportunity comes when we feel we are not ready. But when you choose to serve, you choose to *shine*. Where do you feel called to serve? And how can you be a vessel of service to your family, your community, or the world at large? In yoga we call this service *seva*. Seva is a practice of devotion, selfless service, and love. Serving is how we rise up and align with a greater force and learn to stand in full presence of the goddesses that we are!

MEET GODDESS GAYATRI

The deity I am designating as the goddess of the Crown Chakra is known as the universal divine mother and mother of the Vedas, Gayatri. The Vedas are the most ancient of all yogic texts, dating back to 1500 BCE. Gayatri's name means "myth," "hymn," or "song of wisdom," and she represents the combined strength of three goddesses you have already met—Lakshmi (Second Chakra), Durga (Third Chakra), and Saraswati (Fifth Chakra).[6] She is usually depicted with five heads and is the living manifestation of the most sacred and oldest of all yogic prayers, the Gayatri mantra.

Gayatri Devi is the all-encompassing goddess. She embodies the earth and the sky, all seven chakras, the power of the light within and the divine light above. She sits on a beautiful lotus, the symbol of the chakra system. For our purposes you can imagine her blossoming out of the crown of your head, with the stalk of the lotus growing down through each of your chakras into the ground where it roots itself strongly. This is how she connects heaven to earth. Her five faces refer to the five elements we are all made from (Earth, Water, Fire, Air, and Space); the five senses through which we take in the world; the five *vayus* (the movements of prana); and the five *koshas* (the sheaths or layers of the soul). These layers remind us that we are not one thing, but we have a physical, an energetic, an emotional, a wisdom, and a bliss body. Gayatri is sometimes depicted with ten hands, holding various mudras of protection and blessings along with an arsenal of spiritual weapons.

I have an affinity for all the goddesses in the Hindu pantheon, but Gayatri holds an extra-special place in my heart. It was her mantra that I first learned when I began my yogic journey over twenty years ago, and she has been with me nearly every day since. Chanting her mantra organically became part of my daily life. Gayatri has illuminated not only my path but also my heart. She has shown me and taught me that the light within my own being comes from the same cosmic source and contains the same power as the light of the sun, moon, and the stars above. In this way, she wakes us from our deepest slumber and helps us remember who we really are.

Imagine Gayatri sitting before you now on her blooming lotus, with her five faces beaming with light. She, just like you, is the embodiment of all five elements and all seven chakras, dancing into harmony and form. Breathe in and breathe out her elixir of light. Breathe in and breathe out her divine wisdom, strength, and love.

Allow her to bathe you in the gracious flow of light. You can imagine her light as the combined power and radiance of the sun, the moon, and all of the stars in the sky.

You may choose to play with and repeat the mantra *soma shakti*, which is a mantra I was given many years ago by my teacher Lorin Roche. As you repeat the words aloud or within, ask Gayatri to fill you with overflowing enlightenment and ask her to show you how to share this light and this wisdom with the world. Then notice how you feel.

For your meditation practice this week you will deepen your relationship with Gayatri Devi as you will learn and chant her mantra.

7 DAYS OF DIVINITY

Day One: Altar

As you begin to build your Crown Altar, let yourself be guided by your highest Self to bring this space to life. You may want to include pictures of your teachers, gurus, or guides, as well as symbols of the divine, or forms of light like candles or a lamp. You may choose to make it all white or use all colors of the rainbow. Just remember, there are no wrong choices—your altar is a visual depiction of what divinity, prayer, and freedom mean to you. Go for the feeling that the Crown invokes and allow it to nourish your soul and align you with the divine.

Start with the essentials and then build from there.

Altar Essentials

- Something white, gold, or violet (cloth, crystal, paper, flowers)

- Something that represents the god of your own unique understanding

- Candle

Altar Inspirations

- Pictures of teachers, family, saints, gurus, gods, goddesses you feel connected to
- Something to burn: white sage, palo santo, incense
- Mirror to reflect back your divinity
- Image of Gayatri
- White flowers or purple flowers such as roses, gladiolas, or delphiniums
- Lotus flower (could be a picture, candle holder, jewelry)
- Mala/prayer beads
- Angel cards
- Crystals: selenite, clear quartz, and amethyst
- Oils: frankincense, melissa, Roman chamomile
- Tarot Cards: The Judgment and The Sun

Refer to the Quick Charts in the Appendix for extended meanings of crystals, oils, and tarot cards.

Writing Contemplation

Complete these sentence stems:

1. I am most deeply grateful for _____ _____.

2. Today I can celebrate _____ _____.

3. My gift to myself and the world is _____ _____.

4. I feel that surrender will _____ _____.

5. I receive guidance from Higher Realms in the form of _____ _____.

Day Two: Mudra—Padma

The mudra we are practicing today is called padma mudra. *Padma* is the Sanskrit word for "lotus." As we have learned, the lotus flower is the beloved flower of the chakra system. It is a symbol of beauty, divinity, love, the sacred feminine, and the road we must traverse from the Earth to the Sky to blossom into our fullest potential. The lotus flower, while deeply rooted in the muddy waters, grows out of the darkness and rises up, and flowers open into the light. It invites us to do the same. To honor both the light and dark within, to resist the temptation to spiritually bypass, to not be afraid of our inner depths, to navigate our own murky waters, and to rise up out of our darkness and unfurl into the radiance of our own light.

Here are the step-by-step instructions.

1. Find a comfortable seat in front of your altar. You may also choose to do this practice standing. Ground down into your pelvis and rise up tall through your spine.

2. Supercharge your hands (see page 22 if you need a refresher).

3. Place your palms into anjali (prayer) mudra at your heart.

4. Take 3 deep *nourishing breaths*, inhaling through your nose and exhaling through your mouth. Remember the 360-degree expanse as you breathe into the front and back of your body. The back body represents the unseen, the shadow and all that is hidden here.

5. Keep the heel of your hand, thumb, and pinky fingers sealed together as you allow your palms to open and the other six fingers to gently blossom like the petals of the lotus flower.

6. Soften your gaze and settle it down into the flower you've made with your hands.

7. Take 5 slow, deep breaths.

8. Feel your roots firmly planted and your crown reaching up to the heavens and lift the entire shape overhead. Imagine the 1,008 petals of your lotus flower unfurling as you drink in the rays of divine light.

9. Take at least 5 more slow, deep breaths here. Drink in this light, the nectar of the goddess, until it is overflowing and pouring down into the crown of the head, seeping further into the stalk of the lotus flower, infusing the third eye, throat, heart, solar plexus, sacral center, and base of the spine with the gifts of the divine.

10. When you feel complete, release the mudra by separating your hands and opening your arms wide. Spin the palms down and slowly lower the hands down to rest on your knees.

You can also listen to the how-to audio at www.chakrarituals.com.

Bonus

Try making a *mudra circuit*—begin with your hands in prayer mudra at the heart, blossom the hands open into lotus mudra take the whole shape overhead, open your arms wide, spin your palms down, and gracefully return your hands back to the knees. Repeat this dance 3 to 5 more times blessing the space within you and around you, as you honor the whole of this spiritual journey we are on.

Writing Contemplation

1. What is your relationship with the Divine, with God, Goddess, Higher self, Consciousness, or Source? Is this a relationship you feel you can trust and rely on?

2. How has this relationship evolved throughout this seven-week journey?

3. What does it mean to embrace and accept your own shadow?

The pranayama technique we're practicing for the Crown Chakra serves as a bridge that connects the Earth to the Sky and the Sky to the Earth, through the central channel of you. It combines conscious breathing with simple arm movements. You can think of it as a mini-devotional body prayer honoring the whole of the chakra system. The inhalation, along with its corresponding arm movements, represents the path of *mukti*: liberation, autonomy, and freedom. The exhalation, along with its corresponding arm movements, represents the path of *bhukti*: enjoyment, manifestation, and embodiment. I call this the Breath of Awakening. Let's give it a try.

Following are the step-by-step instructions.

1. Find a comfortable, grounded seat. Feel your roots growing down and your spine rising up.

2. Rest your hands into your lap, with the right palm cradling the back of the left hand.

3. Take a deep, nourishing inhale through the nose. Exhale and sigh it out through the mouth.

4. Bring your awareness to the base of the pelvis. As you inhale, slowly bring your palms together into prayer mudra. Start to trace the pathway of the central channel, with the back of your thumbs lightly brushing each of your chakras all the way up and out through the crown of your head.

5. Once you have reached the crown, hold your breath for a moment, allow the arms to fully extend up and out, and lift your heart to the sky as you turn your gaze up in the direction of the heavens. Before you release the breath, imagine gathering up all of this heavenly energy.

6. As you begin the exhalation, bring your middle fingers to softly touch. With the palms now facing downward, slowly start to press your hands down, like you would a giant coffee press, bringing this awakened consciousness from heaven down through every chakra of your body. At the end of the exhale, return your palms to rest in your lap, just as you began.

7. Continue in the flow of your breath for 6 more rounds.

8. As you flow, feel the wide-open expanse of your being while still feeling your roots firmly planted into the ground. Remember your ground of support as you reach for the sky and remember the vastness of the sky as

you make your descent back down to the earth. With every breath you are opening to more and more freedom, grounding, joy, and possibility as you bring the gifts of the divine down through the vessel of your body—creating heaven on earth.

You can also listen to the how-to audio at www.chakrarituals.com.

Notes

Use slow, deep breaths.

Remember with all pranayamas never to strain.

Do your best to coordinate breath and body movements together.

You can also do Breath of Awakening while standing, which we will explore within the body prayer section.

Writing Contemplation

1. What does *freedom* mean to you?

2. What limitations and constraints have you moved beyond, broken through, and risen above on your pathway to liberation?

3. What within your wild woman's body, mind, heart, and soul still longs to be freed? Make a list and describe what it would feel like to experience true freedom from each item on this list.

Day Four: Sahasrara Body Prayer

Your body prayer for your Crown Chakra is a symbolic gesture of the journey we have travelled together. It will support your continued awakening of consciousness and help you bring that consciousness back down into your body. Allow this final prayer to be an offering to the Highest, whatever that means to you. Do each movement and breath with utter devotion and gratitude for this body and this life.

As always, respect your body and do the best you can.

Suggested use: Repeat the sequence 1 to 3 times on each side. Follow the pictures to come or watch the how-to video at www.chakrarituals.com.

Start standing, feet hip-width apart, knees soft, hands in lotus mudra at your heart.

1. Inhale; arms flow up through lotus mudra. Exhale; coffee press your hands down. Repeat 3 more times

2. Exhale; hinge from your hips and fold forward

3. Step your left foot back. Inhale; rise up into high lunge, sweep your arms up and open

4. Exhale; coffee press your hands down as you bend your back knee. Inhale; flow your arms up through lotus mudra and and restraighten your back leg. Repeat poses 3–4 three more times

5. Exhale; hands down, knees down. Inhale; table pose

6. Exhale; push back to child's pose

7. Interlace fingers, place the crown of the head on the ground and tuck toes

8. Push down into the forearms and elbows, lift hips up overhead, as you straighten your legs. Tap knees down (step 7) and straighten legs 3 times

9. Knees tap down, inhale; flow up through lotus mudra. Extend your arms up and flower them open

10. Exhale, coffee-press your hands down as you sit back onto your heels

11. Exhale; downward-facing dog (step to the top of the mat)

12. Inhale; reach your arms up and open wide. Exhale; hands to lotus mudra

Repeat on the second side, stepping back with the right leg.

Writing Contemplation

1. Write a letter to the divine source, spirit, goddess, or god you believe in. Put your pen to paper and tell your source everything that is troubling you, challenging you at this time. Speak from your heart and let it pour out. Ask any questions you would like to be answered.

2. Once you are complete, close your eyes and take 3 deep *nourishing breaths* and turn to a fresh page in your journal. With your imagination guiding you, listen within and write a letter back to yourself from the divine.

Day Five: Meditation—Shine ON!

Before there was little orphan Annie and her anthem "The Sun Will Come Out Tomorrow," there was the Gayatri mantra. Gayatri is the power and the prayer to the divine light, the energy of activation that awakens us from our deepest slumber and ignorance. It is the energy of breakthrough that illuminates even through the darkest of nights and allows us, along with the sun, to rise and shine yet again. The Gayatri mantra is the sonic embodiment of Gayatri Devi, the mother of the Universe. Within the few sacred syllables, all of the wisdom and the knowledge of the Vedas, the most ancient of all yogic texts, is concealed. That is how omnipotent her mantra is.

Over the years I have heard many interpretations of the Gayatri mantra—here are a few of my favorites. I encourage you to take your time with each one. Read the words slowly, breathe them in and out, feel their resonance, and see what they awaken in you.

"I call upon all the celestial beings of the universe, the earth, the sun, the moon, and the stars. Guide me, show me the way, and help me remember who I am."

—my personal favorite

"Oh Goddess of divine light, bestowing all your blessings, illuminate this path of love and awaken me to live in truth."

—Daphne Tse

"The eternal, earth, air, heaven, that glory, that resplendence of the sun. May we contemplate the brilliance of that light. May the sun inspire our minds."

—Douglas Brooks[7]

For our Crown Chakra meditation practice, we are going to align with this divine intelligence and light by reciting/chanting her mantra. Afraid to chant? Don't worry. Do the best you can and chant with sincerity from your heart. If this mantra is new for you, I strongly suggest you follow along with the audio version here: www.chakrarituals.com.

Here are the instructions for your meditation.

1. Come to a comfortable, seated position at your altar. Ground down into your pelvis and rise up tall through your spine. Feel your connection to both the earth and the sky.

2. Take three deep breaths, inhaling through your nose and exhaling through your mouth.

3. From your heart, begin to repeat after me. We will take the mantra line by line:

   om bhur bhuvah svah (om bhoor bhu-wah swa-ha)

   tat savitur varenyam (tat savi-tur varen-yam)

   bhargo devasya dhimahi (bhar-go de-va-sya dhee mahee)

   dhiyo yo nah prachodayat (dhiyo yo nah pruh chod duh yahhatuh)

4. Continue to recite the mantra for 11 more rounds. As you do so, imagine the light of the divine shining down through your Crown Chakra, awakening your spiritual intelligence, illuminating your vision, empowering your voice, blossoming open your heart, igniting your power, nourishing your womb, and lighting up the pathway of the earth beneath you.

5. *Om bhur bhuvah svah, tat savitur varenyam, bhargo devasya dhimahi, dhiyo yo nah prachodayat.*

6. After the twelfth round, just allow the mantra to dissolve and sit within the effects of its sonic vibration. Turn the corners of the mouth slightly up as you remember your divinity, your power, and your ability to shine. Celebrate the whole of your life. Feel the joy, gratitude, and radiance within your being. May this great golden aura illuminate your mind and, just like the sun on even the cloudiest day does not stop shining, do not hold back your light! Shine on, you radiant Goddess!

Writing Contemplation

1. How does Gayatri and her mantra speak to you? What was your experience with chanting her mantra? How did it feel inside of you?

2. What is enlightenment for you? Define it for yourself.

3. How can I be a channel for source/spirit to work through me?

The embodiment practice for the Crown Chakra was inspired by the positive psychology class I took with Tal Ben-Shahar where he introduced the concept of becoming a Life Connoisseur. A connoisseur by definition is someone who holds a great deal of knowledge, appreciates the finer things, and enjoys life to its fullest. The key to becoming a connoisseur of living is in savoring the moments and experiences of your life. To give yourself permission to indulge by being fully present, by slowing down, putting down the phone, and opting to not multitask. This allows you to welcome your senses to open, to be in awe of the majesty of what is, and—you guessed it—be in the spirit of gratitude. To me, becoming a Life Connoisseur is about falling in love with life (recall that is how Swami Rama defined gratitude) and experiencing the full spectrum of what it means to be a spiritual yet human being. Becoming a connoisseur of anything takes practice; a simple yet beautiful way to practice and awaken to life is through taking *gratitude walks.*

A gratitude walk is just like it sounds—you go on a walk, preferably by yourself; you leave your devices at home; you invite all your senses to join you; and you give thanks. You open your eyes to truly see what surrounds you: the colors, shapes, textures, and the shadows. You open your ears to hear the sounds that surround you; you sip in the tastes and smells as you explore the world around with a full body presence.

I began this practice while in quarantine due to Covid-19. I was feeling isolated, pent up, angry; struggling to write, create, and to feel connected to anything. Being such a visceral person and understanding the power of both movement and nature, the idea of walking while offering thanks appealed to me. I began taking walks every afternoon. With each step I took, I committed to seeing the beauty that was present. It didn't mean I was always happy or that my walk would turn into a skip, but some days it did. I began to notice things I hadn't noticed before—from wild jasmine growing, to the way the sun reflected off the glass buildings and cast a golden aura over the city, to the vibrant works of graffiti art hidden in alleyways, to the smell of the coffee brewing from a neighbor's apartment, to the butterflies literally flying around me. Every time I walked and attuned to the good, a little more stress melted away, and I opened to receive more and therefore had more to give. As I savored each positive experience, I was inviting more love, meaning, and creativity back into my life. In essence, I was re-opening and attuning my connection to divine grace.

Your invitation for this week is to go on at least one gratitude walk. Schedule it into your day. Take at least 15 minutes to slow down, smell, savor, and fall in love with life and let the divine shine in.

Writing Contemplation

1. What was your experience with your first gratitude walk? What did you notice that maybe you hadn't noticed before?

2. How did it differ from walks you have taken before and even from other gratitude practices you may have done?

3. Write one last sincere letter of gratitude to the goddess, universe, or source or whatever higher power you believe in. Thank them for everything they have brought into your life. All the joy, all the love, all the blessings!

Day Seven: Lessons from Your Crown Jewel

- The Rainbow Path leads us to mukti; liberation, and freedom AND bhukti; embodiment, enjoyment, and manifestation.

- Align with the divine. You are part of the great mystery; you are connected to all that is!

- Bravely turn in the direction of your shadow.

- Gratitude is falling in Love with Life.

- Don't put your enlightenment outside of YOU.

- Be a vessel of service for the benefit of all beings everywhere.

- You are a Queen, and you were meant to SHINE!

Today is your day of reflection and rest. Take some time to reflect upon your most important takeaway from this chakra chapter. If there was only one thing you could remember from this chapter, what would it be? Maybe take a moment to note it down as we continue the journey, that one thing that you want to remember. Now is also the perfect opportunity to return back to any of the previous days' exercises or readings.

WILD
WOMAN
MANIFESTO

Congratulations. You've taken the seat of the throne—you've reclaimed your wildness, discovered deeper self-love, connected to the many faces of the goddess, and felt your unbreakable connection to the infinite divine source that runs through all things. As you moved through each chakra, ritual, and body prayer, you rekindled your aliveness and returned to wholeness. And even when you get lost, you now know the path of the Awakened Wild Woman—fully empowered, unafraid to shine, and committed to unleashing the ever-expanding fullness of who you really are.

You are connected both to the earth and the sky, you are shepherded by your inner guidance, you are ready, able, and willing to bring your divine gifts down to the earth. You are a vessel of divine grace. The conduit in which the divine travels from the earth to the sky.

Take a moment to honor this feat, this commitment! Place your hands over your heart and take one deep, *nourishing breath* in and feel the utter gratitude you have for yourself. Thank yourself for showing up and bravely going on this journey of awakening your wild woman. This was no small task. I bow to you now, my wild sister. Tell yourself thank you, tell yourself you love you.

_____[name]_____,I thank you and I love you! Whisper it, sing it, shout it! Allow yourself to feel all that you feel. And then answer these final sentence stems:

What I want to carry forward is _____.

I am most grateful for _____.

The light of the DIVINE _____.

I see the goddess _____.

I can envision _____.

What I choose to create now is _____.

I use the power of my voice to _____.

My heart has room to _____.

My love knows _____.

The flames of my power have ignited _____.

My empowerment allows me _____.

The sacred waters have taught me _____.

My body is _____.

The gift of embodiment has _____.

I am unafraid to _____.

The little girl in me knows _____.

I now remember _____ and I vow to never forget _____
_____.

My wild woman is teaching me _____.

The medicine my wild woman has to offer the world is _____.

What I wish for all women everywhere _____.

I AM _____.

This is the Wild Woman Manifesto, your sacred commitment to the power within you. Put it somewhere you will see it often and read it aloud and often as a reminder of all you have reclaimed, reawakened, and are now committed to. If you feel inspired to share it with your fellow wild sisters, please do—you never know, you might just inspire them to awaken as well. Of course, you have permission to change it as you flow and evolve with your consciousness. Use this Wild Woman Manifesto to remember the journey you have travelled, all you have awakened, and use it as a guiding vision and inspiration for your life.

One of the first things I mentioned to you in this book was that buried inside of you are seven radiant jewels of dynamic power and light ready to be excavated. But to access them you are going to need a very special spiritual map. And now as we end this stage of our journey together, you have not only excavated but have empowered each jewel of intelligence. You now have forever access to this map.

As we each individually do the work to heal and awaken our inner wild woman, we also heal and awaken the collective wild woman. My prayer for all women is that you know you are enough, that you know you are worthy, and that we all—women everywhere—keep lifting each other up.

May you remember your light.

May you remember your power.

And may you always remember that you were born to wear this crown!

Yours,

Cristi

Now that you have completed the seven-week journey and have a basic understanding of the intelligence and empowerments of each chakra, you can go back and use the book intuitively or in a way that works best for you. You might try doing a monthly, weekly, or daily check-in where you ask yourself, *What do I need today?* Is it confidence, courage, grounding, love, clarity of vision, the power of my voice, or intuitive guidance? Tune in and listen for the answer. You may also go the wild woman route and ask, *What quality or qualities of the goddess do I want to embody?* The fearlessness of Kali, the abundance of Lakshmi, the strength of Durga, the luminance of Gayatri, and so forth. Let your answers guide you to the chakras and ritual practices your body, heart, mind, and soul desire to be nourished and supported by. You may choose to work with a single chakra and even a single practice for weeks at a time, or you may choose to work with a different chakra and a different practice every day. Either way play, have fun, and revel in the ecstasy of your own shakti and remember you also have free access to all the audio and video content at chakrarituals.com.

Appendix

CHAKRAS AND CRYSTALS

FIRST CHAKRA	SECOND CHAKRA	THIRD CHAKRA
These crystals ground the body's energy, restore the foundation of all energetic systems, and balance all chakras.	These crystals inspire creativity, encourage a free flow of energy throughout the body, and support emotional balance.	These crystals are empowering, helping to build confidence and courage, and connect to personal power.
Garnet regenerates the foundation of all energetic systems.	**Carnelian** encourages the free flow of energy throughout the body.	**Tiger's eye** builds courage and restores confidence.
Hematite grounds our energy and encourages a feeling of stability.	**Orange calcite** stimulates creativity and positive insights.	**Citrine** enhances powers of manifestation and creation of abundance.
Black tourmaline protects our energy and clears away any negative vibrations.	**Sunstone** helps us connect to our joy and passions.	**Pyrite** attracts positive energy and helps us see our full potential.

FOURTH CHAKRA	FIFTH CHAKRA	SIXTH CHAKRA	SEVENTH CHAKRA
These crystals help open the heart, encouraging unconditional love while clearing away energies that block the heart's expansion.	These crystals encourage heart-centered communication, helping us to listen, speak, and receive information.	These crystals stimulate inner wisdom, helping connect innate intuition with the spiritual knowledge of the Universe.	These crystals enhance our connection to spiritual and universal knowledge, opening our energy to receive new information. They also help harmonize all chakras while encouraging spiritual awakening.
Rose quartz encourages unconditional love for oneself and others.	**Aquamarine** encourages clear, focused communication with oneself, other people, and the spiritual realm.	**Labradorite** provides psychic protection and enhances the connection between inner knowledge and universal wisdom.	**Selenite** connects the Sixth and Seventh Chakras, clearing away blockages and amplifying positive energies of both chakras through purification.
Morganite dissolves the ego and opens the heart.	**Apatite** creates a bridge between the heart and the throat, encouraging emotional expression.	**Lapis Lazuli** helps connect us to our intuition, wisdom, and truth, facilitating our soul's evolution.	**Amethyst** calms the mind and brings about feelings of peace, allowing for the expansion of consciousness.
Aventurine clears away negative emotions from the heart and encourages expansion.	**Chrysocolla** facilitates the sharing of ideas and information, particularly in a group setting.	**Azurite** dissolves conditioned patterns and clears the way for new insights to enter the psyche.	**Clear quartz** balances our entire energetic field, including all seven chakras. It helps connect us directly to the source energy of the Universe.

Created by Jill Wintersteen, the founder of Spirit Daughter, the popular astrology and wellness brand created to help you live your best life. Jill shares inspirational messages to her community of over a million followers on Instagram through @spiritdaughter.

CHAKRAS AND ESSENTIAL OILS

ROOT	SACRAL	SOLAR PLEXUS
Place a drop of your chosen oil on the soles of your feet. Hold gently for a few seconds.	Place one drop of oil an inch below your belly button using your index finger. Hold gently.	Place one drop of oil on the solar plexus with your index finger. Hold gently for a few seconds.
Vetiver grounds us into the present moment.	**Wild orange** connects us to abundance in all areas of our lives.	**Bergamot** helps us to accept ourselves exactly as we are.
Black spruce stabilizes our energy and connects us to a feeling of balanced harmony.	**Jasmine** helps us to establish a harmonious relationship to our passions and desires.	**Melaleuca** reestablishes our energetic boundaries so that we can stay connected to ourselves.
Cassia gives a warming sense of comfort and self-assurance. Dilute with a carrier oil.	**Neroli** helps us to honor meaningful connection with ourselves and others.	**Ginger** reminds us of our innate power.
Affirmation: I am deeply connected to and supported by Mother Earth.	**Affirmation:** Everything I desire comes to me with ease.	**Affirmation:** My power lies in being truly myself.

HEART	THROAT	THIRD EYE	CROWN
Place one drop of oil over your heart space.	Place one drop of oil on your index finger and gently place over your throat/ jugular notch for a few seconds.	Place one drop of oil on your index finger and place it gently on your third eye/forehead.	Place one drop of oil on your index finger and place it on top of your head, holding there lightly for a few seconds.
Geranium reconnects us to love and to our ability to trust in life.	**Lavender** helps us to express ourselves with more ease and honesty.	**Magnolia** connects us to our compassion, which helps us to see things more clearly.	**Melissa** brings light. Apply right before meditation or anytime you want to open yourself to a higher perspective.
Helichrysum helps us to heal emotional pain in our hearts.	**Spearmint** assists us in speaking with confidence and clarity.	**Copaiba** invites clarity and insight.	**Frankincense** awakens you to the truth of who you are.
Ylang ylang revives our connection to our inner child and our sense of wonder.	**Cypress** releases stagnancy, encouraging our thoughts and feelings to flow effortlessly.	**Clary sage** supports us in expanding our vision of what is possible.	**Roman chamomile** reconnects us with our spiritual purpose.
Affirmation: I am safe and loved. I am exactly where I need to be.	**Affirmation:** My voice is a healing medicine for the world.	**Affirmation:** My vision is clear, and I always know what to do next.	**Affirmation:** I am light, and I belong to the source of all things.

Not all sources of essential oils can safely be used topically. Be mindful of the sourcing before applying to skin. Citrus oils are photosensitive, so avoid using bergamot/wild orange on any skin that will be exposed to sunlight. All of the oils can be diluted with a carrier oil as desired.

Created by Elena Brower, mama, student, host of the beloved Practice You podcast, bestselling author, and teacher. Elena's work with essential oils can be found at elenabrower.com. Her yoga and meditation practices can be found at glo.com.

CHAKRAS AND TAROT

	Card	Definition	Affirmation
FIRST CHAKRA	**The Fool**	*A new world welcomes you.*	*I am home.*
	The Empress	*Creation, magical manifestation / woman-i-festation, sacred embodiment*	*I am a powerful creator embodied on Earth.*
	Ace of Earth	*Your body and planet are your home.*	*I am blessed to be alive!*
	Ten of Earth	*Family traditions are your foundation to heal and grow.* *Abundance*	*I am supported by my initial lessons on Earth, and I can create whatever supports me. I am supported by abundance.*

	Card	Definition	Affirmation
SECOND CHAKRA	The Temperance	*Honoring your emotional wounds is the gateway to your loving future.*	*I am serene with all that is.*
	The Moon	*Sacred flow of ancestral wisdom*	*I am part of a sacred lineage that lives through me.*
	Six of Water	*Emotional healing takes time, space, and support; ask for help and receive with an open heart.*	*I am devoted to my healing process and all the joys that will bring.*
	Ace of Fire	*Your sexual ignition and healing reside within.*	*I am a healthy, empowered sexual being with desires and gifts I express freely.*

	Card	Definition	Affirmation
CHAKRA THREE	The Hermit	*First tend to your inner light in order to hold your outer transformation.*	*I honor retreating in order to care for the deeper places within my soul.*
	The Strength	*Live your wholehearted, authentic, and unapologetic life!*	*I am centered in body and soul, where my truth lies.*
	The Tower	*Release limitations, expectations, and obligations to claim your truth!*	*I release it all in order to reveal what's of true value.*
	Three of Fire	*Drop the fear of your power to soar!*	*I am committed to my highest journey, even when the end state is unknown.*

	Card	Definition	Affirmation
CHAKRA FOUR	The Hierophant	*Deep self-care. Reach out for a teacher or healer as you take responsibility for your wisdom, injuries, and healing.*	*I own my wisdom and responsibility to heal.*
	The Lovers	*The choice is yours to find the energy that balances you and honors the path of both individuals.*	*I am powerful and wise and own my choices.*
	The World	*Reunited soulmates hold each other in a balanced and mutually beneficial foundation rooted in love.*	*I am whole, and I choose partnership founded in love.*
	Seven of Water	*Embracing your vulnerability requires deep self-care and awareness. Invest in your mastery of these skills to become a worthy partner.*	*I am responsible for sharing and healing my whole self with compassion and honor.*

	Card	Definition	Affirmation
CHAKRA FIVE	Ace of Air	*Clarification of your thinking, expressive, and inspirational process*	*I am aligned to seeing and thinking in new ways.*
	Four of Air	*Release preconceived, prescribed patterns into your right to Divine downloads.*	*I am a clean slate, open to Divine inspiration and healing.*
	Page of Air	*New mental processing takes roots; allow yourself to be a beginner in claiming your experience and expression.*	*I am learning to express my thinking, my stories, in new, empowering ways.*
	Seven of Fire	*Your inner angst serves as a purification process, uncomfortable and valuable.*	*I am brave and strong. I can stay present for my greater good to unfold.*

	Card	Definition	Affirmation
CHAKRA SIX	**The Magician**	*Claim your Divinely given gifts; cultivate them; share them to strengthen them.*	*I am responsible.*
	The High Priestess	*Your essence knows your magic is powerful, even if the world tries to deny it exists. Devote your consciousness to remembering Life is Magic!*	*I am Magic.*
	Six of Fire	*Focus on your inner guidance to illuminate your next step on the sacred path.*	*I am guided.*
	Eight of Fire	*Your devoted practices keep your inner fires stoked to cultivate contentment and bliss, regardless of judgment and chaos (which is the result of forgotten Divinity).*	*I am connected to the Divine.*

	Card	Definition	Affirmation
CHAKRA SEVEN	**The Judgment**	*Release the mundane, embrace the grace of Divine, which affords our endless renewal.*	*I am Free.*
	The Sun	*Release our Earthly journey of challenges and seeming imperfections; know it's all perfect and it's all the gift of the Divine. Celebrate with gratitude the privilege of being human.*	*I am celebrating my life with gratitude.*

Created by Brenda Rose, who is renowned for her insightful psychic gifts, compassionate heart, and healing presence. Brenda Rose, whose first true love is Tarot, brought forth her Beauty of the Tarot deck, which she's taught from and activated Tarot readers with across the world, inviting exploration of new ideas and new places within, illuminating the path that activates your soul's joy. Visit Brenda-Rose.com, and @TheRealBrendaRose on Instagram.

CHAKRA CHEAT SHEET

Name: *Muladhara*

Meaning: The Root in which all things grow

Physical Location: Root of pelvis, Perineum

Element: Earth

Color: Red

Sense: Smell

Bija Sound: LAM

Vowel Sound: UH

Body parts related: the teeth, the bones, specifically the spine, base of the spine, the legs, the ankles, and feet

Balanced: Grounded, stable, present, able to take care of one's survival needs, feels at home in their body, comfortable in own skin, vital health and wellness, able to let go and relax

Affirmation: I AM Safe. I am Secure. I am at home in my body. I belong here, the earth supports and nourishes me.

Name: *Svadhisthana*

Meaning: Your own sweet place

Physical Location: Sacral center

Element: Water

Color: Orange

Sense: Taste

Bija Sound: VAM

Vowel Sound: OO

Body parts related: hips, sacrum, low back, sex organs, entire reproductive system

Balanced: Emotional intelligence, juicy, sweet, sacred sexuality, ability to go with the flow, fluid graceful movements, life is colorful, vibrant, meaningful, and pleasurable.

Affirmation: I FEEL, I allow my body to be suffused with pleasure, I honor the flow of my emotions, I am in touch and in tune with my sexual power.

Name: *Manipura*

Meaning: City of jewels

Physical Location: Solar plexus

Element: Fire

Color: Golden yellow

Sense: Sight

Bija Sound: RAM

Vowel Sound: OH

Body parts related: Organs of digestion, pancreas, adrenals, liver, core

Balanced: Self-confident, self-motivated, connected to center, aligned with purpose, able to take risks, playful, radiant, says YES to your dreams.

Affirmation: Power Lives in Me.

I say YES!

I reclaim my power now.

I am worthy.

Name: *Anahata*

Meaning: Unstruck, unbeaten, unbreakable

Physical Location: Center of the chest

Element: Air

Color: Green

Sense: Touch

Bija Sound: YAM

Vowel Sound: AH

Body parts related: Heart, lungs, chest, breasts, shoulders, arms, hands, middle to upper back, circulatory, respiratory system, lymphatic system, thymus gland

Balanced: Radical self-love, self-acceptance, compassion, intimate with self and others, good boundaries, empathic, lover of life

Affirmation: I love. I am love, aham prema. I am worthy of love. I love and accept myself completely, I dedicate myself to the path of love.

CHAKRA CHEAT SHEET

Name: *Vishuddhi*

Meaning: Purity and self expression

Physical Location: Throat

Element: Space or sound

Color: Blue

Sense: Hearing

Bija Sound: HAM

Vowel Sound: AI

Body parts related: Throat, vocal cords, cervical spine, ears, jaw, tongue, trachea

Balanced: Speaks authentically from your heart, good listener, honest, true, trustworthy, good rhythm, pacing, timing, embraces and celebrates uniqueness

Affirmation: I speak. I am unique. I am bringing to life my unique and powerful voice. My words matter.

Name: *Ajna*

Meaning: Command, inner illumination, unlimited power

Physical Location: Brow center

Element: Light

Color: Indigo

Sense: Sixth sense

Bija Sound: OM

Vowel Sound: NG

Body parts related: Forehead, eyes, brain, nervous system

Balanced: Strong intuition, clear insight, creative imagination, strong memory, able to manifest

Affirmation: I See. I am magic! I am envisioning, today I expand my scope of vision of what is possible.

Name: *Sahasrara*

Meaning: Lotus of a thousand petals

Physical Location: Crown of the head

Element: Beyond an element

Color: White, violet, gold

Sense: Beyond

Bija Sound: Beyond

Vowel Sound: EE

Body parts related: Crown of the head, skull, cranial bones, cranial nerves, nervous system

Balanced: Experience of inner peace and gratitude, able to see life as a gift, connected to a higher power, feels interconnectedness to all living things

Affirmation: I know. Divinity flows through me. I am FREE! I am one with all of existence.

Love Notes

Now, I have to warn you, this section is going to get a little mushy, as there are so many people I have to thank and honor, as without their love and support you would not be reading this today.

I first want to honor and give reverence to Mother India, to her culture, rituals, prayers, sacred languages, and for all the ancient wisdom teachings of yoga and to all the people of this sacred land whose lives were the creation ground for these practices. I bow down to all my teachers, and their teachers' teachers, as without them we would not have access to this truly transformative gift of the chakra system.

Lorin Roche: Without you, Lorin, there would be no book! There are no words that can truly capture the gratitude and appreciation I hold in my heart for you and for all you have done for me and brought to my life. You have shown me a generosity in your teaching and mentorship that I had never experienced before. It has set the bar for how I want to show up and serve my own students. It's a true honor to call you my teacher, mentor, and friend and to carry on your work in whatever form I can. Thank you for all you have taught and continue to teach me.

Gareth Esersky, my literary agent, and the entire team at Carol Mann Agency. Thank you for saying YES and believing in me and this wild vision of *Chakra Rituals* when it was truly just a vision! Thank you for your extreme patience, for staying the course, for all your wonderful, perfectly timed pep talks, and for your expertise and wisdom!

Daniela Rapp: From our first conversation on the phone, I so hoped it was going to be you and St. Martin's Press that I was going to have the opportunity to work with. Working on this with you has been nothing short of a dream come true. Thank you for this incredible opportunity and for believing and trusting in me, even when I didn't believe in myself!

Fumi James: I know in my heart of hearts that there is no one else in the entire universe who could have brought forth the power of each goddess in such a modern and unique way. The world has never seen anything quite like this! I am blown away by your talent, your creativity, and your mastery. It was truly a joy and an honor to work with you; I am forever grateful and know this is just the beginning!

Seane Corn: I love and respect you more than you know. You have shown up for me at some of the most challenging moments in my life, and this was no exception! Thank you for caring so deeply, for supporting me and truly seeing me. And thank you from the bottom of my heart for saying yes to my big ask and being my first reader!

Justin Michael Williams: Thank you for every word of encouragement, ounce of belief, beautiful and succinct note that you offered, and for every kick in the pants! Most importantly, thank you for helping me see that I could indeed author this book.

Celeste Bolin, Leah Alperin, Peter Johnston—my first readers, thank you so very much for taking the time out of your busy lives to read my manuscript; you each have given me such invaluable and meaningful feedback. It and you truly mean the world to me.

Laura Amazzone: So much of what I know about the Goddess is from what I learned from you. I am so grateful for all the time we have shared, from the countless hours at Exhale Center for Sacred Movement, to the pujas, healing sessions, and talks at your house. And of course, for the trip of a lifetime to Nepal, to the Durga festival, and to the top of Annapurna. *Jai Annapurna MA!*

Anodea Judith: Your work has inspired me endlessly. Thank you for your decades of research, books, teachings, and for your deep devotion and commitment to our beloved chakra system. You have paved the rainbow path for millions around the world, including me.

Elena Brower, Jill Wintersteen, and Brenda Rose, thank you for sharing a peek into your brilliance, wisdom, and gifts to my readers through the creation of your beautiful essential oils, crystals, and tarot charts respectively! I hold so much gratitude and love in my heart for each of you.

JQ Williams: Thank you for your brilliance, your magic, and your Virgo-ness! For your exquisite eye, your patience, for thinking of everything, and for so beautifully bringing the photos of my body prayers to life!

Andy Pettit: Thank you for so generously supporting me in this process of writing my first book. You were like my guardian angel that was by my side from moment one. Thank you for your unwavering patience, your wisdom, and your expertise. It is deeply woven into the pages of this book. From the bottom of my heart, thank you for being my first editor.

To my wild sisters around globe: Ing Ing, Lisa Johnston, Daphne Tse, Elise Joan, Lily Zhang, Shoshanna Kuttner, Toni Bergins, Dearbhla Kelly, Millana Snow, Samantha Mehra, Brenda Kulju, Alexia Kutler, Gaby Aschwanden, Nico Grae, Peggy Santosa, Ginna Christensen, Bettina Eder, Veronica Barcala, and Liz Carey. Each of you are the true embodiment of the Goddess. Thank you for being my light when I couldn't see my own; for being a force and source of inspiration, love, laughter, support; and for showing me the true meaning of sisterhood. Thank you for bravely doing your own work and for bringing your magic to the world and supporting the rise of all women everywhere! I love and honor you!

Leah Alperin, John, and Kennen Nickerson, my quarantine pod as I wrote this book! Thank you for all the love and the laughs you have given me and brought to my life at this wild time. And, of course, for the gift of Hazel! Hazel, thank you for the endless light and inspiration and views. You were the absolute perfect place for me to write this book.

To all the teachers and influences that have touched my life known and unknown, I bow down to you all: Camille Maurine, Anodea Judith, Marianne Williamson, Brenda Rose, Seane Corn, Sianna Sherman, Shiva Rea, Toni Bergins, Sally Kempton, Annie Carpenter, Maty Ezraty, Elisabeth Halfpapp, and my mother and father, Marylou and Hal Christensen.

To Goddess, spirit, my angels, my guides, to the force larger than me that truly brought this book to life! Thank you for birthing *Chakra Rituals* through me.

To every wild woman reading this, I thank you and I love you!

Resources

To access all the free resources from this book, visit chakrarituals.com.

Chakra Ritual crystal kits:

chakrarituals.com/ritualkits and spiritdaughter.com.

To work more closely with me at events, retreats, teacher trainings, or speaking events, visit:

cristichristensen.com

There is nothing I love more than getting to know my readers. Come say hello on social media:
@cristi_christensen

For those of you wanting to go even deeper, I created an Online Chakra Rituals Teacher Training for you!

Available at cristichristensen.com

I have also created several online courses for you, including:

Confidence, Power & Saying Yes!: cristichristensen.com

Core & Cardio: cristichristensen.com

Awaken Your Chakra Connection: udaya.com

Soul Fire Elemental Activation: tintyoga.com

Savor the thrill of aliveness-Chakra Meditations: yogawakeup.com

Elemental Sol Flow: omstars.com

Kirana Yoga School—The global yoga school I co-created in Asia with my partner Ing Ing. *200/500hr Yoga Teacher Trainings*: KiranaYogaSchool.com

Become certified to teach meditation:

Lorin Roche and Camille Maurine, Radiance Sutras Meditation Teacher Training: MeditationTT.com

Additional Goddess Resources:

BOOKS:

The Artist's Way by Julia Cameron. New York: J. P. Tarcher, 1992. (Anything by Julia Cameron)

Awakening Shakti by Sally Kempton. Boulder, CO: Sounds True, 2013.

Goddess Durga and Sacred Female Power by Laura Amazzone. Lanham, MD: Hamilton Books, 2010. lauraamazzone.com.

Meditation Secrets for Women by Camille Maurine.
San Francisco, CA: HarperOne, 2009.

Woman's Power to Heal Through Inner Medicine by
Maya Tiwari

Women Who Run with the Wolves by Clarissa
Pinkola Estés. New York: Ballantine Books, 1992.

The Yoni: Sacred Symbol of Female Creative Power
by Rufus Camphausen.
Rochester, VT: Inner Traditions, 1996.

You Can Heal Your Life by Louise Hay. Hay House
Inc., 1984.

YOGA:

Shiva Rea: www.pranaflow.love

Sianna Sherman: Rasa Yoga & Mythic Yoga Flow
siannasherman.com

Shakti Academy: Women's Empowerment & Yoga
Teacher Training School: shakti-academy.com

DANCE:

JourneyDance™: journeydance.com

MUSIC:

Daphne Tse Music: daphnetse.com

MEDITATION:

Yoga Wakeup: All Bonus content audio recordings
powered by mindful alarm app Yoga Wake Up
(available on iOS and Android, yogawakeup.com)

MAGIC, TAROT, AND INTUITIVE WISDOM:

@TheRealBrendaRose, Brenda-Rose.com

ASTROLOGY, CRYSTALS, AND RITUAL:

@SpiritDaughter, spiritdaughter.com

JEWELRY:

Ananda Soul Creations Jewelry: anandasoul.com

EVENTS:

Burning Man: https://burningman.org

OTHER INCREDIBLE CHAKRA BOOKS AND RESOURCES

The Anatomy of the Chakras,
a course taught by Tias Little.

Anatomy of the Spirit by Caroline Myss.
New York: Harmony Books, 1996.

Chakras and their Archetypes by Ambika Wauters.
Freedom, CA: The Crossing Press, 1997.

*Color Your Chakras: An Interactive Way to
Understand the Energy Centers in the Body*
by Dr. Susan Shumsky

Eastern Body, Western Mind by Anodea Judith.
(Anything by Anodea Judith),
Berkeley, CA: Celestial Arts, 2004.

Llewellyn's Complete Book of Chakras by Cyndi
Dale. Woodbury, Minnesota: Llewellyn
Publications, 2016.

Endnotes

Introduction

1. Dr. Lorin Roche, *The Radiance Sutras* (Louisville, CO: Sounds True, 2014), 8.

1. Chakra Essentials

1. Roche, *The Radiance Sutras*, 206.

2. Roche, *The Radiance Sutras*, 6.

3. Dawn Cartwright, http://www.dawncartwright.com/tantra.php.

2. Ritual Essentials

1. Nancy Olson, "Three Ways That Handwriting with a Pen Positively Affects Your Brain," *ForbesLife,* May 15, 2016, https://www.forbes.com/sites/nancyolson/2016/05/15/three-ways-that-writing-with-a-pen-positively-affects-your-brain/?sh=4d5cec2c5705.

2. Anodea Judith, *Eastern Body Western Mind* (Berkeley, CA: Celestial Arts, 2004), 54.

3. Coming Home to the Root of You: The First Chakra

1. C. E. Finch and J. C. Loehlin, "Environmental Influences That May Precede Fertilization: A First Examination of the Prezygotic Hypothesis from Maternal Age Influences on Twins," *Behavioral Genetics* 28, no. 2 (March 1998): 101, https://doi.org/10.1023/a:1021415823234.

2. Dr. Sará King, The Liberation Experience by Justin Michael Williams Guest Teacher Session titled "Collective shadow" October 2020.

3. Inspired by the teachings of Laura Amazzone, https://www.lauraamazzone.com

4. Your Own Sweet Place: The Second Chakra

1. U. S. Geological Survey, "The Water in You: Water and the Human Body," Water Science School (website), "https://www.usgs.gov/special-topic/water-science-school/science/water-you-water-and-human-body?qt-science_center_objects=0#qt-science_center_objects.

2. Rufus Camphausen, *The Yoni:, Sacred Symbol of Female Creative Power,* (Rochester, VT: Inner Traditions, 1996), 3.

3. Karla McLaren, *The Language of Emotions* (Boulder, CO: Sounds True, 2010), 29.

4. Adapted from the work of Lorin Roche, "Radiance Sutras Meditation Teacher Training Lecture on Desire," delivered in November 2019.

5. Practice inspired by the work of Sianna Sherman and Rasa Yoga, Rasa Yoga Teacher Training www.rasayoga.com.

5. Ignite Your Inner Fire: The Third Chakra

1. Sally Kempton Lecture on the Goddess at Yoga Journal Conference in San Francisco in 2008. https://www.sallykempton.com.

7. You Are Uniquely You: The Fifth Chakra

1. David Marchese, "152 Minutes with the Chief Priestess of Creativity," The Cut, April 6, 2016, https://www.thecut.com/2016/04/julia-cameron-the-artists-way.html.

8. You Are Magic: The Sixth Chakra

1. Cyndi Dale, *Llewellyn's Complete Book of Chakras* (Woodbury, MI: Llewellyn Publications, 2016), 4.

2. Julia Cameron, *The Artist's Way* (New York: J. P. Tarcher, 1992), 3.

9. The Crown Jewel: The Seventh Chakra

1. Robert Augustus Masters, *Spiritual Bypassing* (Berkeley, CA: North Atlantic Books, 2010).

2. Masters, "Spiritual Bypassing: Avoidance in Holy Drag," http://www.robertaugustusmasters.com/spiritual-bypassing/.

3. Ibid.

4. R. A. Emmons and C. M. Shelton, "Gratitude and the Science of Positive Psychology," in *Handbook of Positive Psychology,* ed. C. R. Snyder and Shane J. Lopez (New York: Oxford University Press, 2002), 460.

5. Robert Emmons, "Why Gratitude Is Good," *Greater Good Magazine,* November 16, 2010, https://greatergood.berkeley.edu/article/item/why_gratitude_is_good.

6. Drik Panchang, "Goddess Gayatri," https://www.drikpanchang.com/hindu-goddesses/gayatri/goddess-gayatri.html.

7. Rajanaka, https://rajanaka.com

Index

vagina, 63–64
vayus, 209
Vedas, 156, 209
vigor, 71
Vijnana Bhairava Tantra, xi
vinyasa yoga, 19, 95
   see also body prayers
virgin, becoming, 64–65
Vishuddhi Chakra, *see* Fifth Chakra
Vision Board, 194–96
visualization techniques, 194
voice, 150–53
   chanting, 151–52
   singing, 151
   see also mantras
vulnerability, 129–30, 139

water, element of, 60–62, 90
   ways to connect with, 65
   see also Second Chakra
welcomings and longings of the
   wild woman, 12
Welwood, John, 203
Western medicine, x
wild woman, x, 11
   Kali, 41–43, 55, 183
   longings and welcomings of, 12
   Wild Woman Manifesto,
      225–27
Wilkinson, Laura, 194
will, 94–96
women, x–xi
   anger and, 99

rites of passage and, 65–67
sexuality and, *see* sexuality
Women Who Run with the Wolves
   (Estés), 11
writing contemplation, 21
Wyatt, Marques, 99, 178

yantras, 33
yoga, x, 9, 70
   embodiment and, 20
   vinyasa, 19, 95
   see also body prayers
yoni, 63–65
   mudra, 75–76
Yoni, The (Camphausen), 63–64